"With a map, directions, and the family in the driver's seat, Get Your Loved One Sober *is an important book for any family affected by alcohol abuse.*"

—Claudia Black, Ph.D., author of
It Will Never Happen to Me

"For decades it was believed that there was nothing one could do to help substance-abusing loved ones until they hit bottom or that heavy-handed confrontational tactics were necessary. Bob Meyers has developed a remarkably effective and gentle method for working through family members and concerned significant others to help their 'unmotivated' loved ones get into treatment. It is no longer necessary to feel helpless and hopeless. This book offers clear and practical advice based on solid scientific research."

—William R. Miller, Ph.D., distinguished professor of psychology and psychiatry and author of *Motivational Interviewing*

"Get Your Loved One Sober *is an outstanding resource for persons dealing with loved ones who refuse to get help for their substance abuse problem. Years of research show that the approach described in this book works. I highly recommend it.*"

—Timothy O'Farrell, Ph.D., chief of the Families and Addiction Program, Harvard Medical School, Department of Psychiatry

"If you feel like your life is out of control because of someone else's substance abuse, this book will put you in the driver's seat with research-based strategies that can make life infinitely better—for you and your loved one. Get Your Loved One Sober *fills a void for everyday people as well as professionals who feel helpless and hopeless concerning substance abusers in their lives. Clearly written and engaging, this book can move you from feeling like a passive victim to becoming an empowered, active player in helping a loved one overcome a drinking problem.*"

—Anne M. Fletcher, M.S., R.D., L.D.,
author of *Sober for Good: New Solutions for Drinking Problems—Advice from Those Who Have Succeeded* and recipient of the Research Society on Alcoholism Journalism Award

"*Lucid and clear, this book will help those who love an addicted person find the practical steps they need to take to facilitate change. I recommend it highly.*"

—Thomas Bien, Ph.D.,
coauthor of *Mindful Recovery* and *Finding the Center Within*

Get Your Loved One Sober

Alternatives to Nagging, Pleading, and Threatening

Robert J. Meyers, Ph.D.

Brenda L. Wolfe, Ph.D.

HAZELDEN®

Hazelden
Center City, Minnesota 55012-0176

1-800-328-0094
1-651-213-4590 (Fax)
www.hazelden.org

Library of Congress Cataloging-in-Publication Data
Meyers, Robert J.
    Get your loved one sober : alternatives to nagging, pleading, and
threatening, / Robert J. Meyers, Brenda L. Wolfe.
        p. cm.
    "The program described in this book is based on the Community
Reinforcement and Family Training (CRAFT) therapeutic model"—P. .
    Includes bibliographical references and index.
    ISBN 1-59285-081-2 (paperback)
    1. Alcoholics—Rehabilitation. 2. Alcoholics—Family relationships.
3. Codependency. 4. Change (Psychology) 5. Self-control. 6. Narcotic
addicts—Rehabilitation. 7. Narcotic addicts—Family relationships.
I. Wolfe, Brenda L. II. Title.
HV5278.M28 2004
362.292'3—dc22
                                                            2003057149

08 07 06 05 04   6 5 4 3 2 1

Editor's note
The stories in this book are composites of actual situations. Any re-
semblance to specific persons, living or dead, or specific events is entirely
coincidental.

Cover design by Theresa Gedig
Interior design by Rachel Holscher
Typesetting by Stanton Publication Services, Inc.

Authors' Note

The program described in this book is based on the Community Reinforcement and Family Training (CRAFT) therapeutic model, which has been evaluated in multiple clinical trials (see references) and found to be an effective intervention for the concerned family and friends of substance abusers. Nonetheless, no guarantees, explicit or implied, are given that the reader will experience outcomes similar to those seen in clinical work. This book is not a substitute for therapy.

To those people who have taught me and continue to teach me about the meaning of life: my mother, Evelyn Fritzsche Meyers, my sons, Nicholas Andrew Meyers and Oliver Joseph Meyers, and most of all, my wife and partner, Jane Ellen Smith.

—Bob Meyers, Ph.D.

As always, my work is dedicated to the many teachers who have both instructed me and molded my thinking over the years, and to my family who is my true source of strength.

—Brenda L. Wolfe, Ph.D.

Contents

Acknowledgments

I would like to acknowledge the National Institute on Alcohol Abuse and Alcoholism (NIAAA) and the National Institute on Drug Abuse (NIDA) for their support and encouragement on all the CRAFT research projects. I would also like to thank all the knowledgeable and hard working staff at the Center on Alcoholism, Substance Abuse, and Addictions (CASAA), especially Matt O'Nuska, Roberta Chavez, and Erica Miller. I especially would like to thank my colleague and friend Bill Miller without whom the CRAFT research would have not been possible.

—Bob Meyers, Ph.D.

First and foremost, I wish to acknowledge all the patients who have honored me by allowing me to enter their lives and learn from their experiences. After book learning is done and exams are passed, it is ultimately the patient who creates the clinician. I wish also to acknowledge my coauthor, Robert J. Meyers, for his passion and commitment to this project. If ever there was a soul behind a program, Bob Meyers is the soul of CRAFT. Working with him to offer this effective program to the public is a joyful way to give back to the patient community that has given so generously to me.

—Brenda L. Wolfe, Ph.D.

Can This Book Help You?

If you live with or love someone who drinks or drugs too much, this book can help you. This book offers you a program that has been proven to help people whose lives are affected by a problem drinker, a drug user, or someone who does both. If you feel stuck in a hopeless, substance-ruled life, this book can help you. If you have ever called, or wanted to call, a crisis line, clinic, or hospital and said, "Help, my husband is drinking himself to death" or "Help, my kid stays out all night getting high, and I'm scared to death," this book can help. You will also find help here if alcohol or drugs are destroying your marriage or scaring your children. Whether you are the wife, husband, lover, parent, son, daughter, or friend of an alcoholic or drug user, this book offers you the tools both to help you help your loved one find the path to sobriety and to improve your own life.

Throughout the book you will notice that we primarily illustrate our points with alcohol abusers. The program, however, has been proven to be effective with loved ones who abuse a wide variety of substances ranging from alcohol and marijuana to heroin and crack. Thus, you can effectively apply the program to your loved one regardless of the substance of abuse.

If you have "tried everything" and nothing has worked, but

you are not ready to give up, then you are in the right place. The scientifically validated program on which this book is based has been designed specifically for people who feel they have "tried it all." They have scolded, nagged, begged, bribed, detached, and tried a few tricks not fit to print. Just like you, they love their drinkers enough to keep trying and trying. What they have not done (and what we will teach you to do) is use that love to change the way they and their drinkers interact so that they spend less time feeling miserable and their loved ones discover the pleasure in being sober. From where we sit, that's an awfully good deal. We are confident that you will also find it to be so.

Of course, we cannot guarantee that every single problem will be solved. What we *can* promise is that we will teach you skills to regain control of your life and to offer your drinker the best help available. In some cases, applying these skills does not result in complete abstinence and happily-ever-after—but in most cases, it does result in a better life for you and in sobriety for your drinker. The happily-ever-after is up to you and your loved one to create.

To keep their discussion uncluttered, the authors primarily refer to drinkers for the rest of the book, rather than to drinkers and drug users. The material is equally applicable to both groups, although extra caution should be taken in cases where the user's lifestyle is centered around violence and criminal activity.

A Note from Bob Meyers

For the past twenty-seven years I have devoted my professional life to the study and treatment of substance abuse. As
you might suspect, my interest in this area comes from personal experience. I grew up in a household that was domi-
nated by alcohol abuse. In my home, it was my father who
drank. As far back as I can remember, our family life revolved
around his drunks and my mother's efforts to get him sober.
As you can imagine, life was no picnic. I watched my mother
suffer; she yelled, nagged, pleaded, and threatened—all to no
avail. My dad continued to drink, and I escaped by joining the
navy at seventeen. Sadly, when my mother died at the young
age of forty-five, my dad was still drinking. She never realized
her dream of a "normal" life with him. I have always felt that
his drinking somehow contributed to her early death. My
goal as a scientist and clinician is to help other families avoid
the pain that mine has suffered.

Although my mother was blessed by the support and
comfort she found in Al-Anon meetings,* she was never able

---

*Al-Anon and Nar-Anon are self-help support groups for the friends and
family members of substance abusers. The groups are based on the same
Twelve Step model on which Alcoholics Anonymous (AA) and Narcotics
Anonymous (NA) are based.

to achieve her most cherished goals of getting my father into treatment and getting him to stay sober. It is to her, and the millions of other families that are tortured by substance abuse, that my work and this book are dedicated.

Most substance abuse treatment programs are designed for the individual who is ready to give up his or her substance use. That is, most programs operate on the assumption that the individual has already decided that clean and sober are more attractive than getting high and is now entering treatment to find out how to achieve that goal. If this were true, which it is not, the success rates of these programs would be much more impressive than they are. As it stands, most users refuse to enter treatment and of those who do, most drop out after just a few sessions. Part of the reason for this is that many of the people who enter treatment are there through coercion (court-ordered or threatened with divorce or abandonment, for example) and not because they see a personal benefit to participation. They make the appropriate noises but remain in denial about how their drinking or drug use is preventing them from enjoying a more satisfying life. Thus, they quickly drop out and return to their treatment-resistant stance. What has been missing from the treatment field are programs to teach those of us who love drinkers and drug-abusers to help them see the benefits of treatment, to help them be *ready for* and *open to* change.

Historically there have been few options for those individuals seeking help for treatment-resistant loved ones suffering from substance abuse. Most treatment options either focus exclusively on helping the concerned family member take care of him- or herself or helping him or her talk the user into treatment. In fact, there have been very few programs designed to teach family and friends (we call them Concerned Significant Others, or CSOs) how to encourage their substance abusers to enter treatment. Moreover, until now, there have been no programs that help the CSO take care of him- or herself and teach him or her how to get the drinker into treatment.

The past ten years of my career have focused on developing a treatment program that both helps CSOs improve the quality of their lives and teaches them how to make treatment an attractive option for their substance abusers. Working with other dedicated scientists and clinicians, we have developed a multifaceted program that uses supportive, nonconfrontational methods to engage substance abusers in treatment.

Called Community Reinforcement and Family Training (CRAFT), the program we developed uses scientifically validated behavioral principles to reduce the loved one's substance use and to encourage him or her to seek treatment. Equally important, it assists the CSO in reducing stress and introducing meaningful new sources of satisfaction into his or her own life. The results we have had with CRAFT have been extremely rewarding. Most clients (CSOs) find new joy in their lives from the changes they make for themselves, as well as from the satisfaction of seeing their loved ones begin the journey to healing.

Let me briefly describe some of the research that has supported CRAFT as a successful model of engaging substance users in treatment. In one recent trial funded by the National Institute on Alcohol Abuse and Alcoholism (NIAAA), 130 frustrated family members were randomly assigned to one of three treatment groups (Miller, Meyers, and Tonigan 1999). One treatment group was structured to simulate the type of support and guidance CSOs would traditionally receive from attending Al-Anon meetings. Specifically, it encouraged involvement in the Twelve Step program with the focus on getting the resistant drinkers to enter formal treatment, along with teaching CSOs about denial, detachment with love, and codependency issues (Nowinski 1998). The second treatment group was the Johnson Institute Intervention (Johnson 1986), which prepared the CSO for a confrontational family meeting with the drinker that hopefully would lead him or her to enter a formal treatment program. The third treatment group was CRAFT, which taught the CSOs new strategies for guiding the substance user into treatment at the same time it guided them in attending to their own needs. All three treatments were delivered one-on-one and included up to twelve hours of therapy. The outcomes we were interested in were twofold. Obviously, we wanted to see which approach resulted in the greatest number of loved ones agreeing to enter treatment for their substance abuse. The other outcome of interest was what impact the treatments had on the CSOs' quality of life.

The graph in figure 1 shows the impact of the three treatment approaches on the number of drinkers, initially in denial, who entered treatment. As you can clearly see, CRAFT resulted in approximately two to six times the number of loved ones willingly engaging in an alcohol treatment program. Compared to a 64 percent success rate for CRAFT, the Johnson Institute approach only resulted in three out of ten drinkers in that group engaging, and the Al-Anon approach engaged barely more than one out of ten drinkers.

The impact of the three approaches on the CSOs themselves is equally interesting. In this study we measured depression, anger, family cohesion, family conflict, and relationship happiness. In all cases, we found that at three and six months after treatment, CSOs reported they were much happier, less depressed, less angry, and had more family cohesion and less

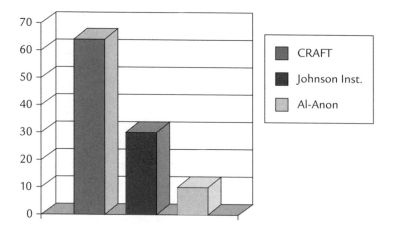

family conflict than prior to treatment (Miller, Meyers, and Tonigan 1999).

Since things worked out so well with the alcohol dependent population, our next step was to evaluate the program with drug abusers (Meyers et al. 1999). The National Institute on Drug Abuse (NIDA) funded a study to determine whether CRAFT would show promise with this population. Everyone who volunteered for the study received CRAFT treatment.

Over the twenty-four months of the study, CSOs whose loved ones were drug-addicted and in denial worked through the CRAFT program. The results were even better than expected. Of the sixty-two CSOs who participated, 74 percent succeeded in engaging their loved ones in treatment. In addition, all CSOs reported significant reductions in anger, anxiety, depression, and negative physical symptoms. Regardless of whether their loved ones entered treatment, the CSOs themselves felt better. As I think back to the pain I watched my mother endure all those years (not to mention my own distress), I cannot help but wish she had had this kind of help. Even if she had not succeeded in dissolving my father's denial, how wonderful if she could at least have learned to take care of her own needs (in spite of him) well enough to enjoy life.

In another study that looked at treatment-resistant drug abusers (Meyers et al. 2002), we randomly assigned family members to one of two types of treatment, each of which were offered in the same clinic and provided twelve individualized treatment hours. One of the treatments was based on Nar-Anon and Al-Anon and emphasized getting the substance abuser into treatment. The second group received CRAFT therapy. Again, there were positive changes in CSO psycho-social functioning. CSOs who learned the CRAFT approach were able to engage their loved ones into treatment at more than double the rate of the comparison approach. In this case, the CRAFT-trained CSOs happily saw 67 percent of their sub-stance abusers enter treatment while the Nar-Anon/Al-Anon group engaged only 29 percent of their loved ones. Our con-clusion, based on the research I have described as well as other studies conducted over the past years, is that CRAFT truly represents a new, effective means of helping people just like you improve the quality of their lives—by developing mean-ingful self-care and seeing their loved ones get the help they need to live more fully.

As of the writing of this book (summer 2003), hundreds of parents, children, husbands, wives, lovers, and friends of substance abusers have enjoyed improvements in their lives by using the CRAFT program. We have seen some incredible changes for the good happen to many wonderful people. For example, worried parents recently came to my office, con-cerned about their thirty-four-year-old daughter who was ad-dicted to heroin. After listening to their description of the many things she was and was not doing that frightened them, I asked them the simple question, "Do you ever say anything nice to you daughter?" At first they were somewhat taken aback, perhaps a little offended, but after some thought they realized that so much of their energy focused on the problems with their daughter that they had lost sight of her positive qualities. Their answer to my question was, "No." After a few sessions of discussing when and how to use positive communications (see chapter 9), they were able to begin a constructive dialogue with her. She was very difficult but eventually agreed to come to ONE treatment session to see what all the fuss was about. We had prearranged to have an appointment occur quickly when she indicated she was ready to come in, and the meeting was very successful. Taking it slow and meeting her where she was (curious but not committed), we talked about the impact of heroin on her life, her relationship with her parents, and her dreams and goals. By the end of the session, she agreed to come back and explore whether treatment was a good idea for her. Her parents wept with joy.

When a middle-aged mother came in for help to get her eighteen-year-old son into treatment for marijuana abuse, she sobbed as she described him. He was a typical rebellious teenager—stubborn, disobedient, and irreverent. His mother had pleaded with him for years to go to therapy but he repeatedly refused. As far as he was concerned, he did not have a problem; the only problem he saw was his mother's nagging. After the mother learned how to map out her behavior and its impact on him (see chapter 2), things started to change. She stopped nagging, pleading, and threatening and changed the way she responded to him to minimize the friction between them. She also learned how to "reward" him for desirable behaviors (like not being high) in a nonconfrontational manner so that their life underwent a metamorphosis from arguments and hurt feelings to relative calm and the reemergence of mutual respect. Mom found that her personal stress levels decreased dramatically—she was able to sleep again, stopped relying on antacids to keep her stomach calm, and returned to the enjoyable activities she had dropped when her son's behavior grabbed all her energy. Most exciting for Mom, however, was when the young man showed up at our clinic for help. When we asked him why he chose to come to treatment at this time, he said, "I guess I just felt like I owed it to my mom. She has been treating me so nice I decided to give it a try." Needless to say, his mother was even more thrilled than were we.

CRAFT has proven itself with the CSOs of individuals who abuse alcohol, marijuana, heroin, amphetamines, and a host of other substances. Thus, although we have written this book to primarily focus on people whose lives are affected by alcohol, you can apply the same methods with loved ones who abuse other drugs. However, if illicit drugs are the problem in your loved one's life, I would encourage you to seek the advice and support of either a therapist or physician. These drugs raise not only legal issues that alcohol (for those over the legal drinking age) does not, but can also negatively affect one's life much more quickly than alcohol on its own. If your loved one is addicted to illicit drugs, you must be especially vigilant about safety issues. Not only do some of these substances trigger violent outbursts that put you directly in harm's way, but they are associated with a drug culture that operates outside the law and often uses physical violence as a means of keeping its members in line. Thus, if your loved one is involved in this lifestyle, you and your dependents may be at serious risk for violence. The risks, moreover, do not stop there. Drug paraphernalia left in the home or anywhere that children may find it spells potential disaster for the children's well-being, and illicit drug use sets your loved one up for being a transmitter of serious diseases such as hepatitis and HIV, among others. Therefore, your loved one's drug abuse potentially targets you for disease. So, as you work through this book and apply the skills you learn to your relationship with your drug-abusing loved one, remember that safety is more difficult to ensure than if your loved one used only alcohol. Apply the same principles but be extra vigilant for danger and be ready to walk away if need be, or to seek outside help.

This book represents the accumulation of all that I have learned over the past three decades and the best of what science has told us is most useful to people whose lives are afflicted by loved ones who abuse alcohol and other drugs. Use it in whatever way will be most helpful to you. You can read it and work through the material on your own or go through it with a friend. A clergyperson, counselor, or psychologist can also help you as you develop new and more satisfying ways of living with your loved one who abuses drugs or alcohol. You are the best judge of what method feels most comfortable to you. Regardless of how you use this book, however, be calm, be patient, and above all be safe.

I wish you good living.

—Bob Meyers

chapter 1

The Program

The subtitle for this book, *Alternatives to Nagging, Pleading, and Threatening,* was chosen deliberately to emphasize that our program offers a positive alternative to the usual tactics people use to try to get their loved ones sober. If your loved one is still abusing alcohol or other drugs, in spite of your repeated efforts to get her to quit, then it is time to try something different. It is time to try the *Alternatives.*

Learning the alternatives to nagging, pleading, and threatening is fairly straightforward. It will not take years of study for you to master these tools. You simply need to work your way through this program and give some serious thought to what you want and to the choices you make. Whether you do that quickly and decisively or slowly and deliberately is entirely up to you. Although the concepts are not complex, your life is, and change will happen at variable speeds despite your consistent efforts. Just keep in mind that if you do not try at all, it is likely nothing will change (at least not for the better). On the other hand, if you use the *Alternatives,* there is the very strong likelihood that your life will improve. Hence, dig in!

The alternative to nagging, pleading, and threatening can be found in a simple system of behavior that has two goals and one central procedure. The goals are (1) to improve the quality of your life and (2) to make sobriety more attractive to your loved one than drinking. The central procedure is something we call "behavioral mapping." It is a way of figuring out how you and your drinker affect each other and how that pattern may be modified to achieve different results. For example, Ruth found it very upsetting that Paul would open a beer as soon as he came home from work every day. In fact, she found it so upsetting that each day she would bitterly complain about it, and they would fight. After mapping out their typical after-work scenario, Ruth realized that her complaints actually made it more likely that Paul would drink. He used the arguments as an excuse to justify his "needing" a relaxing drink. Her nagging also gave him a reason to "punish" her by drinking. Using the same *Alternatives* you will learn, Ruth was able to change her reaction to Paul's after-work beer. Further, by doing so, she eventually made it more enjoyable for him to skip the beer than to drink it. End of beer. End of complaints. End of arguments and punishment. Beginning of a better quality of life for Ruth and a shift toward sobriety for Paul.

Sounds simple, doesn't it? Well it is both simple and difficult. The techniques are not difficult to learn. What can be difficult, however, is applying them in your current life. The way you and your loved one interact is a well-rehearsed routine born of your natural style, his natural style, the impact of alcohol on your loved one's brain and behavior, and the interaction of all of the above. If you think of the changes you want to achieve as a journey, you can draw a parallel between the simple lines on a road map and the techniques you will learn, and then draw a parallel between the actual roads you travel and the life context in which you implement them. Real roads, unlike their clean counterparts on a map, have potholes, detours, and traffic jams. Your life has hard-to-break habits, unforeseen crises, and just plain discouragement that you will need to overcome. However, just as you wouldn't give up a desirable journey simply because some of the roads are bumpy, you won't give up on changing life with your drinker just because it is not always easy. Change is almost never easy; but change for the better is always worth the effort. After months and years of nagging, pleading, and threatening your loved one, you are ready for a change.

A Look Ahead

As we have already said, there are two simple objectives to this program. One is to improve the quality of your life. That means not only getting your loved one to stop abusing alcohol, but more importantly, putting the sanity back into your own life *regardless of whether she ever gives up drinking.* That's right. It is time for your quality of life to become less dependent on whether your loved one is drunk or sober, in a good mood or bad, home or out. To this end, we will help you create a safety plan to ensure that regardless of your drinker's mood, you and those dependent on you do not become victims of violence. (We cover this in chapter 3.) On a happier note, chapter 4 offers you a glimpse of the future you will create. In other words, as you work your way through that chapter, you will figure out what you want your life to look like and begin to translate those dreams into attainable goals. Chapter 5 addresses the guilt that gets in the way of moving forward and helps you feel good about finally being in the driver's seat. Part of moving forward, of course, means rebuilding your emotional and social life. Chapter 6 shows you how.

The objective of moving your loved one toward sobriety, believe it or not, is also helped by improving the quality of your life *independent* of his behavior. As your stress level decreases, you will be able to deal with your drinker in a calmer, less reactive manner, and your relationship will improve. This in turn will help you motivate your drinker toward sobriety.

Unfortunately, your improved attitude, while necessary, is not sufficient to accomplish this second goal. Thus, we also give you a tool kit of techniques that are effective alternatives to nagging, pleading, and threatening. To begin with, the behavioral map we mentioned earlier forms the foundation of almost every strategy. Thus, an entire chapter is devoted to teaching you how to use this important technique. Chapter 2 will explain the behavioral map, provide lots of examples, show you how to use it in your own situations, and help you practice until you can map your interactions and be confident that you really are getting at what triggers your difficulties. Combining this awareness with the other techniques you learn will empower you in a way that nagging, pleading, and threatening never could. Moving on to these other techniques, you will find chapters devoted to disabling your enabling behaviors (chapter 7) as well as useful problem-solving and communication techniques (chapters 8 and 9). "Behavior Basics" (chapter 10) will equip you with the core tools of behavior change so that you can more easily modify your behavior and that of your drinker. (Lest you shudder at the thought of "modifying" anyone, stay calm. The section on page 7 called "A New Angle on Control" will explain what this really means. We are not pushing anything so devilish as mind control!)

Chapter 11 is devoted exclusively to helping you select and support the best treatment approach for your loved one. Chances are you have been down the treatment road before—telling your drinker that treatment will help, begging her to consider it, even getting an agreement to try it, only to have your drinker not keep the appointment or drop out after only one or two visits. In fact, the unhappy reality is that the majority of drinkers who enter treatment seldom remain for more than one or two sessions. However, individuals whose partners, parents, children, and lovers have learned the *Alternatives* stay in treatment six or seven times as long as other drinkers do (Ellis et al. 1992). We attribute this to the fact that our clients learn *how to suggest* and *how to support* treatment. There is more to successfully engaging someone in treatment than guilting or goading this person into it (as you well know). We will teach you how. You will also learn what to do to make staying in treatment as attractive for your loved one as possible.

Finally, chapter 12 addresses the important issues of relapse prevention and what happens after you have done everything you can. As you move through this journey of change, you will experience successes and face obstacles, some minor, others not. However, one of the key advantages of the *Alternatives* approach is that it prepares you to deal with obstacles, potholes, detours—whatever falls in your path. Thus, difficulties become opportunities for you to gain control over your life. Ultimately, whether or not your drinker achieves lasting sobriety, your journey with us will give you the skills and tools to enhance your own quality of life. Hence, in a best-case scenario, the two of you will achieve peace together and worst-case scenario is that you will have done everything possible and be able to move on and take care of your own life. In either case, your future looks brighter.

About Change

As you read this book, keep in mind one important truth. Change is not an event. It is a process—a slow process. No matter what behavior you want to change—a nail-biting habit, overeating, or how you relate to someone—it does not happen in one big jump. Making change is no different than taking a long car trip. You may decide on Monday morning to drive from New York to Los Angeles, but it will take longer than the moment of decision to get you there. You need to pack your bags, figure out what roads to follow, and so on.

What's more, once you start driving, you will find that some of the roads you had planned to travel are closed or in poor repair. You will need to find detours, tolerate potholes, and otherwise adjust your plans as you go. You will also find that if you drive for shorter rather than longer periods each day, the trip will be more enjoyable, and you will feel more rested and in control. The same goes for your change journey.

The improvements you are after will take time and are best achieved in small steps with careful planning. Given how long you have already lived with your drinker under the present circumstances, you can tolerate it a little longer as you make small, controllable changes. Rather than whipping through this book and making a mile-long list of things to "fix," work through the *Alternatives* with the plan of making one small change at a time. As these changes begin to feel natural, go back and add more. What you learn here is yours forever, so you need not hurry up and get through them quickly! Take your time, go slow, and enjoy the knowledge that you are on a life-enhancing journey.

Keep the journey in mind as you move forward. When things don't go smoothly, remind yourself that every road trip has its snags. A highway detour between Albuquerque and Phoenix would not send you scurrying back to New York, so don't give up on your hopes for your drinker just because one or two or more attempts at change hit a wall. Each time you try a new technique and it does not work, sit down and think through what happened. Review your original plan, review what you did, get a clear picture of how your drinker responded, and think about how you might improve your approach. Use the same motivated problem-solving skills you would use if your highway of choice had a detour and you needed an alternate road to Los Angeles. These detours might be a nuisance, but they are a natural part of the journey. Expect them and you will master them.

A New Angle on Control

Only you really know how much blood, sweat, and tears you have invested in this relationship. However, we feel safe betting that you have tried repeatedly to get your loved one to change. Experience shows that when people love someone, they give him the benefit of the doubt, again and again. They keep trying in hopes the individual will finally "see the light" and change. This would be a great strategy except for one problem. Most people try the *same* tactics over and over. The sad thing is they do this not because what they are doing works but because it is the only way they know how. If you think about it, you can see it makes no sense. In fact, it has the same effect as parking yourself in front of that detour on the Albuquerque/Phoenix highway and revving your engine in front of the road-closed sign hoping the noise will force the sign to let you pass. How much more productive it would be if you could pull out a road map and find an alternate route to your destination.

Open yourself up to new ways of interacting with your loved one and have the courage to take control of your situation. Rather than continually knocking your head against the same old walls, come along with us and learn how to control your reactions to your loved one and, through your reactions, shape a change in her behavior.

We are not talking about control in the ugly sense of tricking or forcing someone to do your bidding—that would hardly make for a satisfying relationship. Rather, the control we teach is one you already have but are not using effectively. When you and your loved one get into an argument, you cross-trigger each other's behaviors. For example, let's say your drinker is late to dinner (again!) because he stopped on his way home to have a few drinks at the pub. He is more than a little tipsy but nonetheless in a good mood. You, on the other hand, are furious and let him know what an inconsiderate SOB he is the moment he comes through the door. His mood immediately sours, and he heads for the liquor cabinet and proceeds to get plastered. You throw dinner on the table and spend the rest of the evening alternating between ignoring and scolding him. There might be hope of this "working" except for the fact that the two of you have repeated this scene dozens of times. Clearly, nothing has changed.

Now consider how the evening might have gone if you had greeted him with, "Honey, I feel awful when you come home late and tipsy. Although I love being with you most of the time, I really don't enjoy you when you're drinking. I've already eaten dinner and made plans to go to a movie with my sister. See you later." As you imagine both scenes (the original and our revision), think about the implications of each. In the original, everybody has a lousy evening, and more importantly, your loved one clearly gets the message that even though he is late and drunk, he still gets dinner and he still gets to have you around all evening. While the two of you might be fighting, you are still together. In the revision, you do not give him an excuse to storm over to the liquor cabinet, you avoid all the pain of a lengthy argument, he has to fend for himself for dinner, and he finds himself alone for the evening. *In changing the way you react to him, everything changes.* Of course, this one interaction probably won't trigger him to give up the bottle and begin a new life. But repeated changes like this will nudge him along as he finds it less and less rewarding to be drunk and more and more rewarding to be sober. By changing your behavior, you change your drinker's behavior.

That is the form of control we are talking about. You can learn to manage your behaviors (interaction patterns) to change your partner's behaviors. But it takes courage, work, and patience. Courage to recognize your existing patterns, work to change your behavior, and patience to keep at it until your loved one responds or until you are satisfied you have done all that is possible.

A Taste of Things to Come

Although there is much we have yet to share with you, we imagine you are anxious to begin. Here's an activity to warm you up. On a blank sheet of paper, describe the last argument over alcohol/drugs you and your loved one had. What did your loved one say/do? What did you say/do? Who said what first, second, third, and so on? Write it out as if you were writing a script for a play. Try to capture every nuance. Then look back at the scenario we described above (drinker home late for dinner, spouse angry, subsequent argument). Notice that the nondrinking spouse could change the course of the argument by changing how she responded to the situation. Specifically, the spouse dropped the attack and instead told the drinker how his behavior made her feel. The spouse also made sure the drinker knew he was loved but that his drinking behavior was not.

Now look for points in your argument scenario where you can exert control. Ask yourself whether you are feeding the flames of the argument or possibly reinforcing the behavior that has made you angry. Script a more controlled (softer) response for yourself that makes it difficult for your loved one to keep the argument going. Remember, start with your feelings, show understanding and love, and be clear about the circumstances under which you would be open to being together or discussing the problem. Rehearse this new script in your mind as often as you can. When a similar situation arises again, you will be better prepared to avoid the fireworks.

If you have trouble coming up with alternatives to your

standard routine, don't worry. By the time you finish this program, you will be a pro.

Program Foundation

This program helps you take charge of your part in the relationship. It does not place responsibility for the drinker on your shoulders. *Alternatives* is based on years of scientific research and has proven to be highly effective for many, many people in your situation. The overwhelming majority of our clients' substance-abusing loved ones enter treatment and stay there six or seven times as long as most other substance abusers. Moreover, people who use the *Alternatives* tell us it gives them a sense of hope, understanding, and opportunity. It can help you improve the quality of your life, your relationship, and your loved one's life.

Alternatives is based on the fact that family members and other people who are important to the drinker are the most influential people in the problem drinker's life. Whether in a positive direction or a negative one, the drinker reacts most strongly to those closest to her. As one of those people, you are in a position to steer those reactions in a positive direction. You can have a tremendous impact for good on your loved one. (Think of yourself as both the navigator and the driver. You have the map that shows you which roads are passable *and* you have control of the steering wheel.)

Living with someone for many years gives you an insight into his habits that few others have. In fact, you may know your drinker as well as, or better than, he knows himself. Given that you are motivated and willing to work for what you want, you can make powerful changes. It is the combination of your knowledge and your determination that puts you so firmly in the driver's seat. We will support your efforts by offering you *Alternatives* to whatever strategies have failed you in the past. While there are obviously no guarantees in life, we are confident that you will be able to learn a more effective style of relating with your loved one—a style that will improve your quality of life and increase the likelihood that your drinker will look at sobriety in a new light.

What You Can Expect

Unlike some approaches, we do *not* teach detachment from the person you love. To the contrary, we try in every way to help you make the relationship work. We emphasize education, empowerment, and hope. You will learn to take charge of your life and to develop a better relationship with your loved one. Along with that, however, you will also learn how to ensure a better quality of life for yourself even if, in the end, your drinker chooses to remain drunk. At that point, you will have done everything possible to help her, and you will be ready to let yourself off the hook with a clear conscience.

People who adopt the *Alternatives* experience a variety of results. Some do indeed arrive at the point where they know that letting go is the only way of moving forward. More, however, find that systematically applying the *Alternatives* leads to healthier outcomes. It is not unusual for the road to lead to treatment for the drinker's drinking, and to couple's or family therapy to help work out the differences in the relationship. We have also seen many people make positive changes in their work and social lives—and here we're talking about the drinkers and the people who love them. We focus on a bigger picture than "just" those behaviors involved in drinking; you learn to increase the pleasures in your life and to take care of yourself. As a result, changes in all areas of your life are possible. It all depends on what changes you want and what you are willing to work for. Just as all along Dorothy had the means to return home from Oz (remember the ruby slippers?), you already have the power to change. Now you will learn to harness that power and to make change happen.

By the end of the journey you will see yourself differently. You will be neither the victim nor the culprit in your relationship. You will have taken control of your life, made positive changes, and be in a position to rationally decide where you want to go from there.

Clarisse, whose story follows, learned the *Alternatives* and decided that she wanted to make her marriage work. In spite of what some might see as an impossible situation, she made small, carefully thought-out changes and turned a nightmare into a relationship with a future.

Clarisse and Manuel

By the time Clarisse came to the program to learn the *Alternatives,* she had been in an abusive relationship for more than thirteen years. Her husband, Manuel, made a lot of money, and she took care of the children and ran the house. To the outside world it appeared a happy home. However, Manuel got drunk almost every night and verbally abused Clarisse and the children. He expected her to satisfy his sexual desires regardless of her own feelings and, when she resisted, physically forced her to have sex with him.

It took a few months for her to work up the courage to tell her husband that she was in therapy. She finally told him after he commented that she seemed "less bitchy" lately. He didn't like the idea of her talking to a stranger about their life, but he "let her go" and didn't interfere. Clarisse continued to attend sessions and apply the program techniques. After a number of months, Manuel became curious about the program and was willing to meet her therapist. It was a stormy first meeting, but eventually he voluntarily entered marital counseling with her.

More than a year after Clarisse began learning the *Alterna-*

tives, she and Manuel were still in marital counseling. He had stopped drinking and was working on his relationship with her and the children. She was taking classes at the community college and felt extremely proud of her accomplishments. Clarisse made it clear to her husband that she would never again put up with a relationship that didn't satisfy her needs and the needs of their children. Although it took Clarisse and Manuel longer than is typical to begin making positive changes, their story illustrates how even seemingly impossible situations can be turned around with work, courage, and patience.

Hundreds of parents have also found that implementing the *Alternatives* to nagging and threatening has made a profound difference in their ability to steer their teenagers in positive directions. Rita and Jorge came to us terribly worried about their sixteen-year-old son, Manny, who they had good reason to believe was using marijuana and likely heading down a path that they knew would bring no good.

Rita, Jorge, and Manny

Rita and Jorge were particularly concerned about Manny's increasing tendency to stay out past curfew and sleep through his alarm clock on school days. Worried, Rita searched Manny's room and did indeed find a marijuana pipe and suspicious-looking seeds in his dresser drawer. Rather than blow up at him (her first urge), she and Jorge first gave some careful thought to all of Manny's qualities and behaviors of which they were proud. They figured that if they were going to demand changes in him, they should also be able to let him know what about him was wonderful. They then identified those activities and privileges that they knew were rewarding to him. In particular, Manny loved having use of the family car to take out his girlfriend. Additionally, Manny's girlfriend was a lovely young woman with whom Rita discussed the problem and who told her that she disliked Manny's drug use and had already pleaded with him to stop. Together they agreed that the girl-friend would limit her contact with Manny to times he was straight. If he showed up at her house looking the least high, she would tell him that she really enjoys his company when he's straight and to come back later. For their part, Manny's parents clearly laid out their expectations to Manny regarding curfew and drug use and promised him that honoring curfew, tossing the drug paraphernalia, and showing a "clean" urine each Friday would result in his being allowed to use the car on Saturday nights. At first Manny was angry about the situation, but his parents and girlfriend stood by their plan and he eventually figured out that life was just that much more fun if he complied. As his behavior improved and his parents had more and more opportunities to reinforce him, their discussions became more comfortable and productive.

Book Structure

One of the more difficult aspects of writing this book has been taking the dynamic, interactive process that occurs in therapy and committing it to flat, silent paper. We struggled long and hard with the best way to do this. Should we present this in a 1-2-3 sequence and guide you through everything in the typical sequence of an average client? Or should we just lay everything out in no particular sequence and tell you to pick and choose what looks appealing to you, much as you might select appetizers off a serving tray? Neither of these approaches satisfied us. We rejected the 1-2-3 strategy because we know you are not an average client who needs the typical sequence. You are unique. You bring to the task your personality along with your personal tastes and preferences, skills, and talents. Add to that the uniqueness of your loved one and "typical" is out the window. That left us with the option of offering you a smorgasbord of tips and techniques with no clear direction on when to do what. This was a little more appealing but left us with one problem: if you were already highly skilled at putting strategies together to create productive alternatives to nagging, pleading, and threatening, you would not be reading this book. Thus, we felt we owed you more than an appetizer tray.

As the best possible means of presenting the *Alternatives*, we settled on a combination of the 1-2-3 and smorgasbord approaches. So we've laid out the first three chapters to contain essential components that everybody must understand before they can make any real progress. The remaining chapters provide all the skills and knowledge for which sequence is less critical. As you determine what your next step is, you can apply material from the chapter or chapters that are most relevant at that point in time. We do, however, strongly encourage you to read through everything before you start picking and choosing what to practice. Often a chapter title or section header can lead you to believe you already know or do not need that material when, in fact, the chapter offers a new spin on an old topic—a spin that could do a lot to smooth your road. So take the time to make sure you've packed everything you need, your road maps are up-to-date, and you have a full tank of gas in the car. Don't skip anything.

The easier decision regarding the book structure was to include examples drawn from real people with whom we have worked. To paraphrase an old saying, we believe that one word-picture is worth a thousand instructions. In other words, in each chapter we illustrate the techniques with examples of how other people made use of them. This will help you to see the many ways you can use the *Alternatives* in your life.

Also scattered throughout each of the remaining chapters

are activities for you to do. To help you use each activity to hone your skills, we will show you how the characters from the various case studies complete it. If you are like most people, you will be tempted to read the completed examples and think that knowing what to do is sufficient. Be warned: knowing is not a replacement for doing! If you do not actually work through the activities yourself, the probability of being able to apply the skills is very poor. We strongly encourage you to keep a notebook in which you complete the activities. Some will take only a few moments, and others will make you really think. You will be asked to mull over material you have just read, situations and issues in your life, your dreams, your disappointments—all manner of things. *The purpose behind the activities is to help you really process the material in each chapter and to make it your own.*

As you travel your journey, you will analyze situations and make plans. You will find it most convenient to keep a notebook in which to record your thoughts and plans as well as to organize your activity worksheets. If there is one overriding "fact" in the world of behavior change, it is that people who record important information about their lives are the people most likely to succeed in making important changes in their lives. Set yourself up for success. Work the program by working the activities.

Each chapter will begin with a different case study describing the characters whose activity worksheets within that chapter illustrate our teaching points. At the end of each chapter you will find the ongoing story of Kathy and Jim. They are a fictional couple whose story is a composite of the stories of many real people who have gone through this program. Their story illustrates important points and will help you get a feel for how the *Alternatives* are applied in real-life settings. Although Jim and Kathy are fictional, their experiences are the actual experiences of people who have succeeded with this program.

Kathy and Jim: In Need of an Alternative

Kathy and Jim were childhood sweethearts who married shortly after high school graduation. After eight years of marriage, Kathy entered the program. Their story may be familiar to you.

After high school, Kathy chose to accept Jim's proposal rather than go off to college. Jim quickly got a good, steady-paying job at a local factory, and since most of Jim's high school buddies also stayed in their hometown, he continued to run with the same group. Having been beer-drinking jocks in high school, the guys pretty much continued their tradition of getting together "for a few." Unfortunately, Jim's few became more and more until it got to the point where he paid more attention to drinking than to Kathy.

When they were first married, Jim and Kathy spent a lot of time together—fishing and camping year-round and enjoying their growing family. Over time, though, they stopped doing the activities that initially drew them together. By the time Kathy entered treatment, she told us it had been five years since they had gone fishing or camping, and Jim had completely lost interest in their three children. His only real interest at that point was drinking and hanging out at the bar.

Kathy said she had tried to talk to Jim about helping with the children or around the house, but he said that since he was the breadwinner, it was her duty to take care of the house and kids. She also told us she was afraid to approach Jim about his drinking because the last time she did, he hit her. After that incident, she stayed in the house for two weeks so the neighbors wouldn't see her bruises. She told the kids she had fallen down the stairs.

Kathy was scared and felt stuck. She had passed on her chance to go to college, had never really worked, and didn't see how she could possibly support herself and the children. As for talking to Jim, she was afraid to cross him. She cooked and cleaned and did what a "good wife" was supposed to do, but she became more and more depressed. Kathy gained weight and was ashamed of the way she looked, stopped visiting her friends, and rarely invited family to visit. Holidays became a nightmare for her because she had to be around people and never knew how drunk or how bizarre Jim would act. In her own words, "My life is a total disaster. I feel like dying. If it wasn't for the kids, I'd just run away."

chapter 2

The Road Map

Holly and Dan

Holly came to our clinic after seven years of living, as she put it, "on the edge." When they first married, Dan was what she called a "social drinker," but as he moved up the ladder at work, he began drinking to unwind at the end of the day. "Advertising is a cut-throat business," he always said, and he needed the drink to "de-stress" after work. In spite of repeated suggestions by Holly that he think about looking for other work that would be less stressful and more satisfying, Dan clung tightly to his job, his career aspirations, and the bottle he needed to tolerate it all. As Dan rose higher in the company, his drinking increased. Every day he would come home from work, change into sweats, eat dinner with Holly, and then mix the first of many scotch and waters for the evening. It was then, each evening, that they would argue endlessly. With no children (Holly was afraid to have a baby under these circumstances) and friends long-since turned off by Dan's intensity, there was nothing to do but continue to battle.

In this chapter you will work on three objectives. First, you will map out everything you know about your drinker's drinking patterns. (You will probably be amazed at how much you know.) Then you will use that information to get what we call a "baseline" on her drinking. In other words, we'll help you figure out just how much drinking is actually going on and under what circumstances. Finally, with that information in hand, you will make specific action plans for changing your behavior and, in so doing, changing your drinker's behavior.

Make a Drinking Map

Life with your drinker has given you a tremendous amount of experience and knowledge about his drinking patterns. Each time you think, "I knew he'd do that" or "There she goes *again*," you prove it. You recognize the usual paths your loved one's behavior follows. In fact, there are probably times you feel downright psychic about what he will do next. This knowledge puts you in the unique position of being able to nudge your drinker's behavior in directions you want it to go. First, though, you need a road map. Use your experience to figure out what triggers drinking, what increases and decreases it, where you figure in the mix, and what the booby traps are. In other words, if you want to get to your destination, use a map!

A road map of drinking has three main parts. First, it describes drinking triggers. You can think of these as the highway signs that tell you an exit is coming up. Next, it describes the early signs of intoxication; you can liken this to the reduced speed signs posted on highway exits. Sometimes the intoxication signs are obvious, such as she's got a drink in one hand and is grinning like a moron. Other times you need to use your insight to know whether he's just in a bad mood or whether the highball he stopped for on the way home put him in a foul mood. In other words, you need to recognize the cues that tell you whether your drinker is still moving smoothly down the highway of sobriety or has already turned off at a drinking exit. Finally, the map shows the consequences of drinking. Once your loved one takes that drinking exit, a number of subsequent roads are available. Sometimes what you do in an effort to get your drinker to stop actually makes it more likely that she will drink. That's why it is so important not only to identify triggers and signs but also to map out what happens between the two of you when she drinks. Your map will help you figure out what leads to more drinking and what leads back to the sobriety highway and smooth driving.

Drinking Triggers

Drinking triggers are any events, moods, people, times, days, thoughts, places, or smells that lead your loved one to drink or that warn you that he is about to drink. At the point a trigger occurs, your drinker has not yet taken a drink but you can be pretty sure one is coming. These triggers are comparable to the highway signs that let you know your exit is coming up. Remember, just because a highway sign signals an upcoming exit, it does not always follow that you take that exit. Similarly, something can be a drinking trigger for your loved one even if it does not *always* lead to drinking. The definition of a drinking trigger for our purposes is that it *often* leads to drinking.

Although everyone is unique, some triggers are fairly common, so we have listed them for you in Activity 1. Read down the list and check off those that ring true for your drinker. This will help you see what sort of signs we are after. At the end of the list, add any we missed that apply to your loved one. Try to remember all the circumstances that have often triggered her to drink. Below we have shown you what triggers Holly sees in Dan's drinking road map. Holly first checked the items in Activity 1 that rang a bell with her. Then she reviewed them, thought through them, and summarized and individualized them to Dan's typical pattern. Study her activity and then do your own in your notebook.

Activity 1. Drinking Triggers

Which of these often trigger drinking by your loved one?

	Boredom
X	Bad day at work
	Good day at work
X	Any day at work
X	Nervous feelings
	Depression
	Riding home from work with friends
	Watching sports with friends
	Watching sports alone
	Children annoying or irritating him/her
	Argument with you
	Feeling good and wanting to celebrate
	Having friends over
	Looking for something to argue over
	Premenstrual syndrome (PMS)
X	Complains about his/her boss
X	Gripes about co-workers
	Mopes around the house
X	Overly full schedule
	Talks about how hopeless life is
	Kids are noisy (or, at least, the drinker complains they are)

What triggers have we missed that typically lead your loved one to drink? Add them to the list and then summarize everything to reflect your loved one's typical pattern. Holly has summarized Dan's pattern below.

Dan's Drinking Pattern

Dan has a high-stress job, which for most people does not automatically lead to drinking, but for him is definitely a drinking trigger. He often feels inadequate at work and worries that one day he will be "found out" for the "fake" he feels he is. Thus, whenever project deadlines are coming due (as they do quickly and often in advertising), or Dan has to give a presentation where he feels he will be evaluated, his stress level goes through the roof.

Over the years of listening to Dan's reports about work and watching his evening drinking bouts, Holly has identified the following drinking triggers. Note that in Dan's case, they all revolve around stress over being evaluated.

Dan's Drinking Triggers

- *Project deadline due within three weeks*
- *Dan has to give a presentation to a client with his boss present*
- *Company functions (picnics, golf tournaments, parties, etc.) in which Dan will be socializing with people above him in the hierarchy*
- *Comments by co-workers that lead Dan to believe that someone else might be given an assignment he wants*
- *Anytime Dan comes home and says it was a "cut-throat" day*

(We know that many drinkers don't need a specific "trigger" to start drinking. However, you can usually find a pattern that frequently precedes heaving drinking.)

◆

Drinking Signs

Now that you have a rough picture of what sends your drinker in search of a drink, think about how you know he has already had one. Between the first swallow and being drunk, there are usually signs that tell you someone is moving from sober to drunk. Once alcohol hits the brain, the time for reasoning and negotiating is past. Liquor and other drugs almost immediately interfere with a person's ability to think clearly. At that point, you have only two objectives. The first and most important is to remain safe. If your loved one is showing any signs of violence, you need to implement your safety plan (see chapter 3). If safety is not an issue, your second objective becomes prime and that is to do nothing to encourage further drinking. The behavioral maps you develop will show you how to achieve this second goal.

What changes as your loved one begins to drink? Does he start pacing? Do her eyelids droop? Does he start looking for something to pick a fight over? Review the list in Activity 2 and add any signs we missed that signal a drinking episode has begun. If you have trouble with this exercise, try tracing backward from her last drunk and figuring out what happened or what she looked like each step of the way.

Holly described Dan's drinking signs like this. Study her activity and then complete Activity 2 for your loved one in your notebook.

◆ Activity 2. Drinking Signs

I know my loved one has started drinking when she or he . . .

	Brings home a twelve-pack
X	Clenches his/her jaw or fists
	Begins to get glassy-eyed
	Gets droopy eyelids
X	Starts speaking more loudly or softly
X	Says she/he works hard and deserves at least one
	Gets morose
	Begins to slur his/her speech
	Becomes more emotional
X	Paces around our home
	Becomes less emotional
	Withdraws from me and/or the family
	Insists the children have "quality time" with him/her even if the kids are busy doing something else
	Wants to be left alone
	Has fierce mood swings
	Refuses to eat

Think about other signs that your loved one is on the way to a drunk. List them and then summarize it all to reflect your loved one's typical pattern. Holly has summarized Dan's pattern below.

Dan's Drinking Signs

Dan goes through periods when he tries not to let me see him start drinking because he knows how upset I get. When he does that, he'll often stop for a drink on the way home or offer to run an errand after dinner and stop in at Joe's Pub while he's out. Even if I can't smell the liquor on his breath, I can tell when he's done this by the following signs:

- *His voice gets louder.*
- *He clenches his jaw.*
- *His tie is loosened. (He never loosens it until he gets home if he's sober; ruins his image he says.)*
- *He forgets to take off his shoes when he comes in, and he always takes off his shoes if he's sober.*
- *He keeps going to the fridge as if he's looking for something to eat but nothing appeals to him.*
- *He complains that no one at work appreciates his talents.*

Good job. You now have a pretty good picture of what situations are high-risk for drinking (that is, drinking triggers) and what signs your drinker sends as he takes that drinking exit. This completes the first and second parts of the map.

Drinking Consequences

The final part of the map outlines the consequences of drinking. The more specifically you can identify a step-by-step sequence that ends in drinking or in drinking-related problems, the easier it will be to figure out how to change that pattern.

What are the results of your loved one's drinking? Depressing as this exercise may be, without it your map will be incomplete and so will be your ability to change your situation.

Sit back for a moment and think about all the consequences caused by your loved one's drinking. Be sure to consider not only the immediate consequences such as arguments and hangovers, but also the long-term negative consequences such as financial debts, medical problems, missed opportunities, and lost friends. While you're at it, also think about any positive consequences you experience from her drinking. Odd as that sounds, it is possible that your loved one's drinking serves some useful role in your life. Perhaps it allows you to avoid an unsatisfying sexual relationship or keeps your drinker dependent on you. We're not saying there *has* to be a positive consequence—only that you need to honestly consider the possibility so that you don't get blindsided by it as you start making changes. Remember, knowledge is power.

Holly was able to identify consequences of Dan's drinking that she had not thought about before. Becoming aware of them helped her figure out what to change and how.

Use Activity 3 to start your own list of drinking consequences. Remember to think both long term and short term, as well as about costs to your drinker and to you. Here is Holly's work on the activity. Do your own activity in your notebook.

◆ Activity 3. Drinking Consequences

	Drinking has caused me or my loved one to . . .
	Feel sick
X	Have bad hangovers
	Feel guilty or shameful
X	Miss work
	Be more socially outgoing at parties

	Be fired from work
X	Lose pleasure in our relationship
	Struggle with raising the children
	Have car accidents
	Get arrested for drunk driving
	Have financial difficulties
	Experience physical problems
	Experience or fear domestic violence
	Be embarrassed by drinking behavior
X	Be unable to relax
	Engage in unsafe behavior (for example, driving too fast or driving while drunk)
	Lose friends
	Become less physically attractive
	Have to live with a damaged or lost social life
	Develop a bad reputation in the community
	Have weight problems
X	Not be able to have sex
X	Have an inhibited sexual relationship
	Have a less inhibited sexual relationship
X	Have my or our possessions broken
	Feel we'd never split up because my drinker needs me
X	Avoid dealing with other problems because we're always dealing with drinking
X	Avoid an unsatisfying sexual relationship

Think about other consequences of drinking that matter to you. List them and then summarize the whole set to reflect your situation. Holly has summarized her situation below.

Dan's Drinking Consequences

I always thought that Dan's drinking basically caused our arguments and not much more. Of course, I worried about what problems it would cause in the future but didn't really think it was doing much damage at this point. When I sat down and thought about it, though, I realized there were many more consequences than I realized.

- *Arguments (obvious)*
- *My migraine headaches (more frequent and severe when he's drinking)*
- *Occasional missed work—Dan with a hangover, me with a migraine*
- *Dan gets out of helping with dinner clean-up and evening chores like paying bills and taking out the trash*
- *It allows us to avoid discussing whether to have children (Dan really wants to, but I'm not sure I want to interrupt my career)*
- *Our sex life is almost completely dead*
- *Dan gets clumsy and breaks glasses*

◆

Let's look at Holly and Dan to put together what we have covered so far.

Holly identified Dan's drinking triggers as work-related situations that make him feel he will be evaluated and come up short. These are the "cut-throat" days to which Dan refers. Holly also identified signs that Dan has already had a drink and is heading for a drunk. When Dan arrives home with his tie loosened and his jaw clenched, she knows he has left work a little early and stopped at the local bar to have a drink. The set of his jaw also tells her he is not about to be talked out of another drink (there is no point in trying to have a rational conversation with someone who's brain is under the influence of a drug). The consequences for Dan and Holly are probably familiar to you: arguments, anger, resentment, loss of intimacy, angry words that sting long after the silence begins, broken glass as Dan gets clumsy, and missed days of work for both of them (Dan with hangovers and Holly with migraines and sadness).

Your most important task at this point is to make sure you can identify your loved one's drinking triggers, can tell when he has started drinking, and know what the consequences will most likely be. With that information on hand, you can begin to make changes. Just as Holly can tell when Dan comes home primed for liquor and arguments, you can tell when your loved one is heading down that road. Knowing this, you can choose not to go there. Instead of engaging in the same old dance of arguments and tears, take note of the triggers and signs and change the consequences that are within your control. You can remove yourself from the situation, change what you say, how you look, and what you do. You will see as we go along that there really is a lot you can change.

Get a Baseline

"Baseline" simply means the place from which you start. Getting a baseline on your drinker means estimating as best you can how much and how often she drinks. In other words, describe her current drinking patterns. There are two reasons to establish a baseline. One is to complete the map that describes everything you know about your loved one's drinking, and the other is to help you recognize progress as it happens.

How Much Does Your Loved One Drink?

The first step in getting a baseline is figuring out how often and how much your loved one drinks. Use Activity 4 to do this. Think carefully and try to answer every question. If you have trouble getting a clear picture of his drinking, use a calendar and think back day by day. Did she drink yesterday and, if so, how much? How about the day before and the day before that? Does your drinker tend to drink less/more during the week or weekend, or does the pattern change each week? If he has a fairly standard pattern of drinking, this exercise will be easier to do but, in either case, it is important.

Almost every drinker has "special drinking days" on which she tends to really indulge. Depending on your drinker, special drinking days might be holidays, paydays, Super Bowl Sunday (or any Sunday), Stanley Cup play-offs, birthdays, Friday nights, or any other day that serves as an excuse to pull out the stopper.

If you know your loved one drinks more than you can observe or if you think he drinks more than you know about, go with your instincts. Many problem drinkers sneak drinks, so you're probably right. At any rate, you can't monitor her activities twenty-four hours a day so use your best estimate.

As you answer the questions in Activity 4, use the following drink definition as a guideline. Each of the following counts as one drink:

12 ounces of beer
4 ounces of wine
1-¼ ounces of 80-proof liquor
1 ounce of 100-proof liquor

Each of these quantities contains ½ ounce of ethanol, which is the chemical in alcohol that makes it a drug.

Activity 4. Estimate Drinking during a Typical Week

Note: If your drinker does not work a standard Monday through Friday week, adjust the activity accordingly.

1. *How many drinks does he/she usually drink on a typical Monday, Tuesday, Wednesday, and Thursday? Multiply the usual daily intake by 4.* _____
2. *How many drinks does he/she usually drink on a typical Friday?* _____
3. *How many drinks does he/she usually drink on a typical Saturday?* _____

4. How many drinks does he/she usually drink on a typical Sunday? _____

5. Add up your answers to questions 1, 2, 3, and 4. _____

The total you entered on line 5 reflects the number of drinks during a typical week for your loved one. Compare this number to your estimate of his typical drinking a year ago, three years ago, or when you first met. Has this number increased over the years? Does the number of drinks go up or down on special days—holidays, vacations, other special times?

You can also estimate how many hours each day are spent drinking or in alcohol-related activities. Time spent going to liquor stores, in bars, being hungover, and stuck in jail or the hospital is part of the drinking pattern and costs. Also add to your baseline any other drugs your loved one may use. A detailed picture of where you are today is knowledge that will help you get to where you want to be tomorrow. Repeat this exercise periodically as you implement the *Alternatives*. Changes in these numbers will be one means of measuring the impact of your efforts on your drinker. Remember, though, even if your loved one does not move toward sobriety, the more important measure of success will be an improved quality of life for yourself and those who depend on you.

How Much Is Too Much?

Even without the detailed exercise you just completed, we are sure you have argued with your loved one about how much she drinks. You have claimed it is too much, and your drinker, very likely, has argued it is not much at all. Sure as you may be most of the time that he does overdrink, there probably also have been times when you wondered who's crazy. After all, you do know other people who drink as much as your loved one. Also, there are probably times she drinks less and you wonder whether you are making too big a deal out of it. What is normal drinking anyway?

There are many definitions of normal drinking and of problem drinking. In fact, gather a group of substance-abuse experts in a room and you'll be entertained by the circus! We'd rather not worry about how many ounces of which alcohol is "officially" too much. The definition that we find the most useful with real people is: *If an individual's alcohol intake is causing problems, that person is drinking too much.*

We also tend not to bother labeling anyone as an alcoholic. Aside from the inability of experts to agree on exactly who merits this title, "alcoholic" is a stigmatized label that has driven many a drinker from treatment. If your drinker is willing to make the effort to quit, is it also necessary to label your loved one?

Take a Deep Breath

Highlighting the extent of the problem as you just did can be pretty upsetting. This may have been the first time you really identified the full impact of alcohol on your life—and it may be worse than you had realized. So stop, take a deep breath, and remember that documenting the problem has not changed anything. Your loved one drinks no more or less than before. You are now simply aware of it and ready to take it on. With a complete drinking map, you can start figuring out how to add smooth, healthy roads to the terrain.

Redesign the Map

Redesigning the drinking map means rearranging the way you interact with your drinker to eliminate or minimize the triggers that lead to drinking. Instead of watching your drinker go from one drinking episode to the next, you will build new roads that go from old drinking triggers to new nondrinking activities. To illustrate what we mean, let us tell you about Ed and Lydia.

Ed and Lydia

Ed had been trying for years to get Lydia to cut back on her drinking, but nothing worked. Nagging, pleading, threatening, cajoling—everything fell on deaf ears. Lydia wasn't a "falling-down drunk" as she put it and wasn't about to give up something that made her feel so good so fast when she got stressed. Ed, on the other hand, saw Lydia's drinking as a major problem since it resulted in her missing work, forgetting to pick up their kids from day care, and once driving home with the kids when she was drunk. Ed finally tried a different approach. He disengaged from the battle and, instead, mapped her drinking behavior and his responses to it (just as you have done). He then outlined new behaviors for himself that would, in turn, elicit different behaviors from Lydia. For instance, when Lydia would come home from work complaining about the unfair treatment she received from her boss (a known drinking trigger), Ed would rub her shoulders and tell her how much he and the kids appreciated her even if her boss was a jerk. Then he'd tell her to enjoy a hot bath while he prepared dinner and make it clear to her that he really enjoys being with her when she is sober. Knowing that baths were one of her favorite stress-busters (next to liquor), Ed was able to sidetrack Lydia from the wine bottle long enough to defuse her mood, get dinner on the table, and shift her attention to more pleasant topics. The more often Ed was able to do this, the more positive experiences he and Lydia shared after work, and the more likely Lydia was to leave work anticipating feeling good when she got home. This positive anticipation, in turn, helped to defuse much of her work stress and made it easier for her to not drink.

You can re-map your drinker's behavior, like Ed did, using the information you have gathered in this chapter. To do that, examine your loved one's drinking triggers and target the two or three most common ones to begin with. For each one, describe everything you know about it: all the details of the trigger itself (who, what, where, when, why, how) and every consequence including how you and others react to what goes on. Also, describe what the drinking pattern looks like—does it begin with "only one" drink and slowly continue until the drinker is plastered, or does your loved one drink with fury, hard and fast?

The easiest way to re-map your drinker's behavior is by drawing it out on a piece of paper as Ed has done with Lydia in the following example. Use arrows to show how one event leads to the next.

Lydia comes home complaining. → Ed points out he had a rough day too, and the kids clamor for attention. → Lydia pours herself a drink while beginning to organize dinner. → Ed asks her if she's going to get drunk again. → Lydia tells him to lay off and knocks back the first drink while she continues fixing dinner. → Ed tells her what a poor example she is for the kids. → Lydia pours another. → Ed storms out of the kitchen. → The children start crying. → Lydia, having put something on the stove to heat, pours another and heads to the bedroom to change out of her work clothes. → Ed follows her in and apologizes. → She accepts but is now a little tipsy. → Lydia heads back to the kitchen and refills her glass two or three more times. → By the time dinner is ready and the family is gathered around the table, Lydia is drunk, Ed is furious, and the evening is a disaster.

Once Ed mapped out the sequence that follows Lydia's lousy-interaction-with-her-boss trigger, he could figure out how to interrupt it. In this case, he knew that the trigger was more than just a lousy day at work. The real trigger was the stress Lydia was feeling. So he decided to interrupt the sequence by introducing some stress reduction right at the beginning. When Lydia came home upset, instead of pointing out that everyone has rough days at work (so stop feeling sorry for yourself), he focused on helping her relax. It's true that he had to take on some extra work in terms of fixing dinner himself and keeping the kids from jumping her for attention, but he had a good payoff. Lydia stayed sober, and they were able to enjoy the evening together.

Before we look at Ed's revised map, it is important to stress that we are not suggesting you permanently take on all the work of the relationship. Indeed, the long-term goals here are that you have less work to do in keeping the family running and that your loved one becomes an involved, responsible family member. Between then and now, however, you will need to put out extra effort. Besides, our guess is that you are already doing most of the work anyhow. This is a continuation of that state of affairs but with a better long-term outcome.

Now, here's what Ed's revised map looked like. The old paths are in *(italics and parentheses)* and the new behaviors are shown in **boldface**.

Lydia comes home complaining. ➔ *(Ed points out he had a rough day too, and the kids clamor for attention.)* **Rub her shoulders and tell her how much the kids and I appreciate her. Tell her to take a bath while I fix dinner. Also tell her that the bath will help her relax without a drink so our evening can be more enjoyable.** ➔ *(Lydia pours herself a drink while beginning to organize dinner.)* **Lydia takes a bath while I fix dinner.** ➔ *(Ed asks her if she's going to get drunk again. ➔ Lydia tells him to lay off and knocks back the first drink while she continues fixing* *dinner.* → *Ed tells her what a poor example she is for the kids.* → *Lydia pours another.* → *Ed storms out of the kitchen.* → *The children start crying.* → *Lydia, having put something on the stove to heat, pours another and heads to the bedroom to change out of her work clothes.* → *Ed follows her in and apologizes.* → *She accepts but is now a little tipsy.* → *Lydia heads back to the kitchen and refills her glass two or three more times.* → *By the time dinner is ready and the family is gathered round the table, Lydia is drunk, Ed is furious, and the evening is a disaster.)* **Lydia comes downstairs relaxed, and we enjoy dinner.**

Examine your drinker's map for the most troublesome or common trigger and ask yourself if it might be covering the real trigger, as it was in Lydia's case. Don't get too deep with this, though. Often, things really are what they seem. If carpooling from work with his drinking buddies on paydays is a trigger for your drinker, chances are that really is the trigger, and you need to focus on finding some other way to get your loved one home from work. You might try offering to pick him up yourself and take him out to dinner (at a restaurant without a liquor license). That way you not only help him avoid a strong drinking trigger but replace the drinking behavior with a healthy, enjoyable alternative.

Revise the map of the triggers you have selected, being careful to draw the complete current map and then to add detours at every point where you can change something. Keep in mind, as well, that if your first detour doesn't work, it helps to have a second detour planned for subsequent points in the sequence. In Ed's case, if the shoulder rub and bath had not worked, he might have planned an understanding reply (see chapter 9) to Lydia's complaints and had a backup plan of suggesting they all go out to dinner, having carefully selected a restaurant that had a children's menu and no liquor license. This way, Lydia would be pulled quickly into an activity that was relaxing and alcohol free.

While chatting over dinner, it would also be helpful if Ed could help Lydia change her focus. Rather than dwelling on what a jerk her boss is or putting herself down for deserving his nasty comments, Ed could help her focus on something positive going on with the children or on a vacation they are planning. The idea here is simply to defuse the situation by changing from a negative topic to a positive topic.

As you plan, make sure you don't keep driving in the same old rut. If the methods you've been using in the past have not worked, chances are they won't work now. Look for new non-confrontational ways to achieve your goals (see chapter 9). Remember, too, the goal is not to prove your drinker wrong and you right (satisfying as that may be). Your goal is to deal with this drinking problem and build a better life. Don't fight your *drinker*. Fight the *problem*.

Changing the pattern from the point after the first drink requires extra caution. As always, the most important objective is to remain safe. If your loved one has any tendency to turn violent, make sure to work through chapter 3 before you make any changes. Don't be a martyr. If your loved one shows signs of turning mean, drop the subject, back off, and, if necessary, leave the premises. Remember that alcohol changes the way the brain works, so anything you do after the drinking starts should focus on your behavior and getting you out of an undesirable situation. Do not waste your time arguing, negotiating, or discussing with an alcohol-infected brain.

You know the signs of early intoxication as well as those of flat-out plastered. Plastered is better left alone as there is little available brain function for you to appeal to. Just having started drinking, however, may be somewhat more manageable. For example, if you get home from work to find your loved one got there ahead of you and is already showing her typical "I've had a few" squint, you have a choice. You can follow the traditional map of asking her if she's been drinking (obvious) and letting her know how disappointed, angry, and hurt you are. From there, the two of you can have your traditional fight, she'll drink her traditional fill, and the day will end in its traditional mess. On the other hand, you can have a new map ready to follow and improve the chances that the evening will turn out well. Consider the following scene.

Mom: Hi, Honey. How did your day go?

Eric: It sucked. I had a horrible day. I'm just glad it's over.

Mom: I'm sorry you had a rough day. Would you like to go out for dinner?

Eric: No. I just want to relax and wind down. I need another drink.

Mom: Why don't I put on a pot of coffee and make an omelet [his favorite meal]. Anything special you want in it?

Eric: Yes, I want some ham and green peppers. I'm starving.

In this case, things worked out well for Mom and Eric. She acknowledged his mood and offered him a nondrinking way to improve it. She didn't get involved in an argument over whether he should be drinking, so she did not become part of the problem. Mom offered a solution. However, things don't always work out that well. Let's look at how it might have gone poorly, but not horribly, for Mom and Eric.

Mom: Hi. How did your day go?

Eric: It was a long, insufferable day, and I'm glad it's finally over.

Mom:	I'm sorry it was so rough. Would like to go out and get a bite to eat?
Eric:	No, thanks. I just want to be left alone and have a drink.
Mom:	I could make us some supper, anything you like. Just say the word.
Eric:	I said the word. Leave me alone. I want to drink in peace.
Mom:	I can see that you don't want me around, and I'd rather not watch you drink. I'm going to take a bath and go to sleep early. I hope you feel better. I'll see you in the morning.

Notice how in this version, Mom gives Eric his space. She began by trying to be sympathetic and offer him a non-drinking solution, but he was determined to follow a drinking path. So, rather than getting into it with him and becoming part of the problem, Mom wisely opted to remove herself from the situation and do something nice for herself by taking a bath and getting a good night's sleep. If she had stayed in the situation, the tension would have escalated and not only would nothing have been solved that night, but both of them would have been too angry to talk in the morning. This way, Eric got his way, Mom had a better night than if she had stayed, and they could attempt a reasonable conversation the next day.

Don't overwhelm yourself with re-mapping all of your drinker's behavior patterns. You've lived with the problem this long; there is no need to solve it all in a day. In fact, trying to do so will only burn you out. This is a new way of living, so take your time and ease into it. Change is a journey, not an event. It doesn't happen overnight. It happens over time.

Selecting the road maps you want to begin with can be

tough. There are so many areas of your life that hurt. However, our recommendation is to start with a fairly specific typical interaction that upsets you. For example, you and your loved one may have a nightly argument over whether to drink in front of the kids or how late he sits up surfing the Internet and drinking. Pick something that is fairly contained—not an ongoing situation such as continually being mean to one another. Also be sure to select an interaction that is at least partially within your control. The arguments your loved one gets into with other people are not fixable by you. The arguments the two of you get into are.

Now that you have identified your loved one's drinking triggers, signs, and consequences at baseline, you are ready to start drawing your map. Activities 5 and 6 show you how Holly took all the information she had about Dan's drinking and created two versions of her road map: one version describes where she and Dan typically end up and another describes where she wants to go.

The chapters that follow will give you many techniques to use in your new behavior maps. For now, plan the changes you can and then read on to see what new approaches can help you design more powerful road maps.

Activity 5. The Old Map

Dan arrives home clearly having had a few drinks. ➔ Holly points out that he is two hours late for supper and begins banging pots and pans as she serves his meal. ➔ Dan tells her to knock it off. He's had a hard day. ➔ Holly feels her temper flare as she snaps, "I work too, you know. My day was no picnic, and you should have called." ➔ Dan yells, "I told you to back off. I'm out of here." He leaves to go back to the bar. ➔ Holly spends the rest of the evening washing dishes and crying.

emergency exit plan, by learning to identify early warning signs of violence, and by changing behavior to short circuit the violence." If we had just told you to do your best to reduce the risk of violence in your family, we would have been of little help to you. By writing chapter 3 to match the very specific goal we just described, we were able to clearly show you what to do.

"Reduce the Emotional Stress in My Life"

This category gives rise to a tremendous range of possible goals, so you will need to think carefully about what needs to change to reduce your stress. You may find that what you list in this category will be achieved by goals in other categories. For instance, freedom from fear of violence, which is addressed by goals in the "reduce violence" category, will eliminate some stress. Similarly, if being able to rely on your loved one to come home from work sober and in time for dinner is a stress-buster, you may have already taken care of this with other goals you have set. Undoubtedly, some stress-reducing changes are not covered in other categories of goals. Examples would include such goals as "incorporate more enjoyable socializing into my lifestyle by rejoining my quilting club," or "reduce my tension headaches by learning a portable relaxation technique."

Before you try to generate a goal to reduce the emotional stress in your life, review the different areas of your life for stressors. Think about your relationship with your drinker, other family members, your work, social life, and health behaviors. Once you have a reasonably complete picture of what is causing your stress, then you can figure out what would be most effective to focus on and what you can change.

"Get My Loved One into Treatment"

If you have been struggling with this situation for a long time, you have probably spent your share of time wishing the problem would just go away. You may have even gone to great lengths to try to "cure" your loved one on your own. However, the fact that you are reading this book tells us that the problem is still here. It also tells us that you are ready to take the next step. That step, in our opinion, is treatment.

We will talk at length about treatment in chapter 11. For now, we will just focus on the idea of getting your drinker into treatment. And there are almost as many ways of trying to do that as there are drinkers. You can try (or may have already tried) nagging, pleading, threatening, cajoling, coercing, blackmailing, seducing, beseeching, and plain old begging. You can also try using the relationship you already have with your drinker to gently make her want to change because there are more benefits to changing than remaining drunk. This last method is the one we teach and the one scientific research has shown to be most effective. Thus, as you define the goal that will help your wish of getting your drinker into treatment come true, consider this goal statement: "By changing the way I interact with my drinker, I will help him come to the decision that entering treatment will improve his life." What you learn by working your way through this book is designed to help you achieve this goal.

"Learn How to Support My Loved One's Sobriety and Treatment"

This may be a new concept for you. Not many people have thought about what it means to *support* treatment or sobriety. In spite of the fact that you are not the cause of your drinker's problems, the relationship the two of you have developed over time may help perpetuate the drinking. Thus, if the drinker enters treatment or achieves sobriety but the relationship doesn't change, remaining sober may be more difficult than necessary. Other than making the commitment to do so, leave the goal setting for this objective until you read chapter 11. When we talk about helping your drinker into treatment, we will also talk about ways you can stack the deck in favor of her remaining in treatment long enough to achieve sobriety.

The categories of wishes and goals we discussed here are the ones we see most often in clinical work. However, you may have other objectives you want to achieve. Our not having mentioned them does not mean they are unimportant. To the contrary, the goals that matter to you are the *only* important ones. Use Activity 11 to map out the goals you want to achieve over the next few months.

◆ Activity 11. Goals

In your notebook write down the goals you want to achieve for each category listed below. You can see in the examples provided how Mark was very specific about what he wanted to make happen. Be as specific as possible and don't worry if goals overlap between categories. No one is grading this. As long as you understand what you are working toward and what matters to you, it is perfect.

Help my loved one get sober

I want to learn how to talk to Maria about her drinking without a fight. I want to figure out whether there is a good time to approach her and exactly how to begin the conversation. I want to be able to enjoy her again.

Reduce the risk of violence in my family

I want to learn how to stop Maria's temper outbursts before they get out of control and she begins to throw things. I want to learn how to keep my temper under control so I don't feed the fire.

Reduce the emotional stress in my life

I want to go to work without worrying about Maria. I also want to make some time just to do things I enjoy—either with her, other friends, or by myself. It's been too long since I've done anything other than worry and pick up after her.

Get my loved one into treatment

I want to figure out how to talk to Maria about entering treatment without it turning into an argument (I think I'm repeating myself now but this is really important). I want to learn more about alcohol problems so I can help her. I want to figure out what I've been doing wrong so far.

Learn how to support my loved one's sobriety and treatment

I need to learn how I can help make treatment and quitting as easy for her as possible. There must be something I can do to help once she agrees to quit. Also, I need to make sure I don't do anything to hurt her chances.

Others . . .

I want our relationship to have more shared enjoyable activities and fewer arguments once she quits drinking. I don't want her to get sober and then hate me for forcing her into it. I guess this goal is about everything. I want our life to be good. So I need to learn as much as I can about the process of quitting and relapse prevention so I can make sure my actions make it easier for her to stay sober.

An Important Point

Before we continue our journey, we need to make an important point. After the intensity of thinking about everything you want to change, you are probably feeling a little overwhelmed. You have a lot of work ahead of you. The important point we want to make is: *Relax. You are on your way.* You have already made some tough decisions. It is important for you to remind yourself of your progress and to appreciate just how much effort it takes. Even the goal-setting exercise we just went through is nothing to sneeze at. Not everyone has it in them to take inventory of their life and map out a course for change. You are special in your willingness to go out on a limb and try to make life better. You will get there. The road is a tough one, but you have a good road map and the commitment to use it. Take it one step at a time and things will gradually, but surely, come together for you.

Priorities

This program is about you. As much as helping your drinker is a priority, it is essential to keep in mind that *you* are at the center of everything. You are the one who suffers because of his drinking. You are the one who keeps the family together. You are the one who covers up, picks up, and sticks up for the drinker. You are the one who has had enough. You are the one who most wants change, and you are the one who is making it happen. That means, in this whole topsy-turvy mess, *you are the most important player.*

As you think about your goals, keep in mind that to accomplish them, you need to have the energy and heart to keep going. *To make sure you do, you absolutely must take care of yourself.* In most cases, that means placing the goals related to your personal health and welfare high on the list. *In fact, experience has taught us that the most effective helpers are those who help themselves first.*

Look over the goals you outlined in Activity 11 and place a great big star beside those that tend to your needs. Perhaps you set goals to increase your enjoyment by joining a bowling team or planning a get-together with your cousin, or perhaps you have decided that exercise has been missing from your life for too long and you will begin walking again. As the tugs and tussles of living with your drinker unfold, keep your eye on your priorities; take care of yourself so that you can help both of you. In the midst of trying to help your problem drinker, do not lose yourself.

Dream On!

In the face of all the goal setting and planning associated with this program, it is sometimes easy to lose sight of the bigger picture of how you want to feel. That is, all those behaviors you want your drinker to do more or less of, all those changes you want to make happen; they are all part of your dream. You want the pain to go away. And you want more than that. You want to feel good, know love, and enjoy life. It is important to stay in touch with that dream.

After you read this section, close your eyes and think about your relationship with the drinker in the old days—back when life was good. If the drinker is your spouse, you may think back to a time when you were dating and trying to impress one another. You remember those times—buying gifts, happily doing what the other person wanted to do, romantic dinners or walks in the park, passionate sex. Remember the excitement of a new relationship? Think about how you felt. Do you remember the warm feelings? The sense of hope and future? Do you remember how you couldn't wait to see one another, spend time together, no matter when or where? Also think about the plans for the future you once had. Can you envision what your relationship was going to be? Remember these expectations and how it all seemed so possible.

If you are a parent of a drinker, remember the dreams you had for your child, the aspirations, the life you still want for her. You may have other children who are doing great, or maybe you know a nephew or a niece or a close friend's child who is living the kind of life you want for your drinking child. Use these thoughts to help you recall the hopes you once had. We know that as a parent you want the best for your children. What are those dreams?

In Activity 12 you will take these thoughts and write them down. Write them one at a time and be as specific and positive as you can. For example, you may have anticipated that you and your loved one would be spending quality time together, maybe dining out, socializing with friends, or going to the movies.

◆ Activity 12. My Perfect Life

Describe your vision of a perfect relationship. As you write, be clear and positive. For example, "I want to have more fun with him or her; we never have fun anymore" is both vague and negative. It doesn't define fun and makes a negative statement by describing what doesn't happen rather than what you want to happen. You could rewrite this example to make it upbeat and specific. "I would like it if once a week Sal would take me to the movies, and once a week we could go out to eat somewhere nice." Another specific, positive example might be, "I'd also like Sal and me to spend some time without the children so we can be more relaxed and less distracted." Read how Mark completed the activity. Notice that it isn't superspecific at this point. He is outlining a vision for where he wants to go. As he progresses, he will make his vision more specific so that what he needs to do will become clearer, and he will have a strong sense of his progress. Write your description of a perfect relationship in your notebook.

I would like Maria to stop drinking altogether. I would like for she and I to go out to the movies and dinner at least a couple of times a month like we used to. I'd like to take walks in the park and have a healthy social life like we used to. I want us to visit family and friends and go to church socials. I want to be able to tell Maria my feelings

*and have her talk to me about hers. I would like to work together on
our financial plan. I want to discuss having a family of our own and
what that means to her. I want us both to work in jobs that are
rewarding.*

As you work through Activity 12, remember this is the "perfect" situation, so don't be shy about what you want. You are
describing your dream, and no rule anywhere says that dreams
must be sensible. Write down as many thoughts, desires, activities, and behaviors that you can think of that you would like to
change in your relationship. The only requirement is that you
phrase everything specifically and positively. Each of us creates
our own reality, but first we have to visualize it. So dream on.

---◆

Action Summary

You laid important ground in this chapter. After you have
put this book aside for a little while, reexamine your goals
and double-check them for two things. First, make sure they
really do matter to you, and second, make sure they are specific. Rework them if the thought of achieving them does
not truly excite you. It will be especially important to have
highly desired goals as you move forward because at times
you will have to bite your tongue or be courageous to achieve
them.

Recap

- Set specific, meaningful goals for your relationship.
- Make sure the destination you are working toward
  is one that is appealing enough to keep you going

through all the ups and downs of the change journey.

Kathy and Jim: Creating the Future

When Kathy and Jim first got married, they were the "perfect" couple. She loved his playful spirit and sense of adventure, and he loved her quick mind and compassionate nature. There was little they did not enjoy doing together. They would go to the movies or out with friends almost every weekend and often spent the weeknights curled up on the sofa together watching television or listening to music. Camping, fishing, and just plain laughing were a big part of their lives.

As Jim's drinking increased, however, their time together deteriorated, and Kathy found herself alone more and more. She also found herself spending a huge amount of time trying to come up with schemes to get Jim to cut back on his drinking. She threw out liquor that he brought home, "forgot" to give him phone messages from his drinking pals, hid his car keys so he couldn't go out, and invested a great deal of her breath pleading with Jim to let their life together go back to the way it used to be. Needless to say, she got nowhere. In fact, Jim complained that she was always on his case and he didn't know what she wanted anyway. All her effort just made him withdraw further into the bottle.

It wasn't until Kathy took a long, hard look at what she was doing and clarified her goals that things began to change. Instead of pleading with Jim to be more like he used to be, Kathy clarified in her own mind exactly what it was she missed. She made a list of the things they used to do together that she wanted him to do now and the things he does now that she wanted him to stop. She was careful to describe each one in a very positive, clear fashion. Rather than telling Jim she wanted him to be affectionate like he used to be, she told him she wanted him to "spend an evening or two each week watching television or listening to music with her." Similarly, rather than telling him to be less critical of the kids, she asked him to say one loving or complimentary thing to each child each day "because they look up to you and it makes them want to behave better." (Notice how Kathy managed to compliment Jim at the same time she asked him to praise the children.)

Once Kathy knew exactly what she wanted Jim to do, it was much easier for her to find effective and positive ways to communicate that to him. As she dreamed about the future she wanted with Jim, Kathy was able to select and modify her specific goals to help create that future. Each time Kathy avoided an argument or refrained from fixing things for Jim, she knew they were moving in the right direction. Although Jim didn't immediately hop on the bandwagon of change, he did notice that Kathy had stopped nagging and that their time together was more enjoyable than it had been. Shortly after Kathy changed her style, Jim even commented that she seemed to be "less of a pain these days." It may not have been the type of compliment he used to give her, but it was most certainly better than the names he had been calling her a few short weeks before. At that point, Kathy knew they had a future.

chapter 5

The Driver's Seat

John and Mom

In spite of her reservations about his readiness to be on his own, John's mother agreed to help him rent his own apartment during his freshman year at college. She was proud of his good grades and outgoing personality, although she also worried about his taste for parties and alcohol. Over the course of the school year, it became increasingly apparent that John's taste for partying was beginning to interfere with his ability to keep up his grades and hold on to the part-time job that paid part of his living expenses. By winter break Mom pulled the money plug and John moved home. Unfortunately, he brought his new lifestyle with him. The atmosphere at home became increasingly hostile, with arguments and yelling the dominant communications between John and his mother.

Taking the driver's seat requires that you do two things. One is that you believe you have the *right* to drive. The other is that you believe you have the *power* to steer.

The Right to Drive

Sometimes the most powerful way to help someone you love is by stepping back and taking care of yourself. Think about it. If you are angry, frightened, or depressed, how effectively do you really think you can help anyone? It takes a lot of energy to remain calm and think clearly when you feel angry, frightened, or depressed—and calm, clear thinking is exactly what is needed where alcohol abuse is concerned. The drug pretty much makes it impossible for the drinker to be rational. If you sacrifice your own well-being to take care only of the drinker, who remains to help the relationship?

If someone's drinking problem has eaten away at your self-respect and confidence, you are not alone. This is a common result of loving a drinker. People whose lives feel out of control automatically look for something or someone to blame. Your drinker is no different. So the more he loses control, the more he needs someone to blame. Unfortunately, the easiest target for blame is the person closest to him. In this case, that's you. Undoubtedly you have been the target of accusations such as, "If you didn't nag me so much, I wouldn't drink," or "You just don't understand." Month after month and year after year these interactions wear away at your self-esteem until you begin to almost believe *you* are the problem. When that happens, your own misery adds to that already created by the drinking problem, and your ability to help the situation basically goes down the drain like last night's ice cubes.

Stop blaming yourself. Regardless of what the drinker (or anyone else) may have told you, someone else's drinking cannot be your fault. Yes, your behaviors have an effect on the whole drinking lifestyle picture, but *you did not cause this person to become an alcohol abuser.* All people have stressors in their lives, some more harsh than others. But not everybody copes by getting drunk. Even if you are not the perfect wife, husband, father, mother, son, daughter, aunt, uncle, niece, nephew, lover, or friend, you cannot be the cause of someone's drinking. For whatever variety of reasons, the drinker responds to life by drinking. She could just as likely have turned out to be someone who responds by sleeping, eating, or meditating. We are only at the beginning stages of understanding why people respond the way they do. The one thing we can be sure of is that *you did not cause the problem, and you must not pay for it.* In fact, the sooner you stop paying and start taking care of yourself, the sooner you will have the energy to focus on interacting with your drinker in a more positive way. That will help you move your drinker toward wanting to become sober as well as help you find a happier way to live for yourself, your drinker, and your family. If you really love your drinker, show it by loving yourself.

You are not the problem, but you can be part of the solution. Get the facts, place the responsibility where it belongs, and learn to accept happiness.

Proof Positive: It's Not Your Fault!

Are any of these thoughts familiar to you? *I just don't know how to help him. If I were a better husband . . . If only I didn't go to work when he was so young . . . If I were a better daughter . . . Other people help their loved ones, why can't I?* Chances are that these sorts of thoughts have gone through your mind at some time or another. When you spend months or years in a troubled relationship, it is natural to begin to doubt yourself. Furthermore, if you compound this natural inclination with the drinker's accusations and the subtle and not-so-subtle accusations from others, it is almost impossible not to feel guilty. Think back to what your loved one was like before all this started. Remember how her drinking became progressively worse. Think about what changed. Can you recall how your loved one's drinking escalated? Remember how the problems associated with drinking also got worse—moods became erratic and hard to predict and shared enjoyment dropped off.

Are you spending less and less good time together? If your loved one is also your lover, have you stopped looking forward to sex? Is your drinker angry most of the time and blaming you for his troubles?

These next questions are the tough ones so think hard. Did you want all these negative things to happen? Did you ask your loved one to drink more and more until alcohol began to rule her life? Did you force your loved one to drink? Did all your friends become problem drinkers? Do you enjoy having alcohol be such a central factor in your life? Of course not. You did not ask for this. You did not work for this. You did not cause this.

You can only take the blame for something you caused. Your having a relationship with this person did not cause him to become a problem drinker. Everyone responds to life's stressors differently. Some people take up yoga or jogging, others kick their dogs, some snarl at the world—and some drink. Each person's response is a little different. Your loved one responds to life by drinking. If she were not in a relationship with you, there would be another person or situation on which to blame the drinking. The bottom line, though, is that you can take neither the credit nor the blame for it. It is time to let yourself off the hook. You are living with the problem, but you are not the cause of it.

You Have the Power

Taking control, steering the relationship so to speak, is within your power. As you work on your behavioral maps, you will begin to see that you have the power. As you see it, you will begin to believe it.

It is often easier to see our own behavior patterns if we first learn to identify them in others. Carefully study the following scenario and the two reactions that follow.

John comes home from school late and drunk and tells Mom he had car trouble. She knows all too well that he was drinking and his car is working fine. Mom is sick and tired of his lame excuses and . . .

Reaction #1	Reaction #2
. . . tells him so. She yells at him and accuses him of being a liar. John screams that she's a hysterical witch and slams out of the house. Mom knows he is going to drink some more.	. . . decides she's not going to take it anymore. She says, "John, we both know you haven't been at school all this time, and I am hurt that you are lying to me. When you've slept it off, I want us to talk about this. In the meantime, I'm going to bed. Good night." As Mom walks out of the room, John flops onto the sofa and turns on the television.

As you can see, in Reaction #1 Mom basically poured gas on the fire. John came home drunk and already defensive (if he wasn't on the defense, he wouldn't have to lie), and Mom's reaction triggered a pretty violent reaction. By blowing up, she made it easy for him to react as he did. Thus, while she may have felt better about "speaking her mind," she did nothing to improve their relationship, change his drinking, or improve her own life. Indeed, if yelling and nagging were effective at changing behavior, John would have stopped drinking the day he moved home.

Reaction #2 shows an equally powerful effect of Mom's behavior on John. Only in this case, she triggered a non-combative reaction. By remaining calm and letting John know how she felt (as opposed to pointing out what was wrong with him), she got her message across and avoided escalating the interaction into another fight and another excuse for him to continue drinking. Of course, John could have opted to return to the tavern anyhow, but in that situation it would have been tougher to blame his behavior on Mom.

Just as Mom's behavior affects John's behavior differently, depending on how she reacts to him, your behavior can have a positive, negative, or neutral effect on your loved one's behavior. Use Activity 13 to explore the ways your behavior can influence your drinker's behavior. As you complete the third section, think about remaining calm and clearheaded during the interaction, avoiding confrontation *(not to be confused with avoiding the issues)* and not accepting responsibility for the drinker's behavior. Also, look for positive, rather than negative, ways to phrase your communication. For example, if you want your spouse to take off his muddy boots before entering the house, a negative request might sound like this: "Honey, I hate it when you wear your dirty boots in the house. Please take them off before you come in." A positive request turns that message around so that the listener hears a loving statement in the request to change: "Honey, I really appreciate it when you take off your boots before coming into the house. It makes my job of cleaning much easier." Difficult as it sometimes may be to reinforce someone who has not put nearly the amount of energy into the relationship that you have, remember that you catch more flies with honey than with vinegar. If you want the person to be receptive to your prodding for change, keep the interaction positive.

In Activity 13 we ask you to analyze how you could decrease the likelihood your loved one behaves in undesirable ways. Before doing the exercise, however, take a look at how Marge's husband figured out how he could affect her behavior.

Describe something your loved one does that really upsets you and that you would like him or her to stop doing.

Marge wakes up in the morning with a severe hangover after drinking all night. She drags around the house and grumbles about how she's too ill to help with the kids or housework.

Describe what you might do that would make it more likely your drinker would do the behavior you just described or make the situation worse.

I punish the behavior by not talking to her. The more she talks or tries to apologize, the more I walk away and say nothing. She gets really mad and usually ends up heading out the door for a drink.

Describe what you might do that would make it less likely your drinker would do the behavior you just described or make the situation better.

I could say, "You know I disapprove of your drinking and staying out all night, but I do want to hear what you have to say. I also want you to know that when you are feeling better, I am willing to discuss it with you fully, but right now you seem to be a little under the weather and I am still too angry to discuss last night with you. Let's talk at supper."

In the second response, Marge's husband makes his feelings known and also lets her know that he is willing to discuss the situation, but at a time when they are both in better condition to do so. It calmly shows concern but doesn't discount the severity of the situation. In addition, by remaining calm and delaying the discussion until both are in better shape, it gives the partner a chance to regroup and make plans about how to discuss the situation. It allows him to be proactive instead of reactive—always the better position to be in if you want to retain control and increase the likelihood you will achieve your goal, whatever it may be.

The example below uses one of Mark's entries in Activity 10 (chapter 4). You can model your plan on his if it helps. Read the activity and write your answers in your notebook.

Activity 13. Behaviors with Power

Step 1: Copy one of your entries from Activity 10 (in chapter 4), Step B here.

Makes fun of me when I ask her not to drink.

Step 2: Describe what you might do that would make it more likely your drinker would do the behavior you just described or make the situation worse. (You can probably draw from real life experience here.)

If I get defensive or try to argue with her. If I try to explain that someone has to keep it together and take care of the house. Sometimes I tell her I just want to do something to help her, and then she really gets pissed off. If I start to cry, she picks on me more.

Step 3: Describe what you might do that would make it less likely your drinker would do the behavior you just described or make the situation better.

Sometimes when I get angry, I just walk away. She usually doesn't follow me; she just shuts up. I never bring up her mom, but maybe if I mentioned what she'd say if she saw her picking on me, it would make her stop. Worth a try.

Congratulations, you have just designed your first "behavioral intervention." That's a big phrase that basically means you planned behaviors (yours) that will intentionally change someone else's (your drinker's) behavior in the desired direction. You now know how you can make the situation you described in Activity 13 worse and how you can make it better.

Below is another completed Activity 13. Examine the responses by Harris's partner, along with our commentary, to see what you can learn.

Describe something your loved one does that really upsets you and that you would like him or her to stop doing.

Whenever we go out to dinner with my sister and her husband, Harris keeps knocking back gin and tonics until he gets pretty loud and obnoxious. He ends up embarrassing everybody. A couple of times we've even been asked to leave the restaurant.

Describe what you might do that would make it more likely your drinker would do the behavior you just described or make the situation worse.

We've been through this so many times that it really pulls my trigger. I end up yelling, more of a loud stage whisper given the setting, something along the lines of, "Don't you dare order another drink. You're embarrassing me again." This usually ticks him off and he orders a double.

Describe what you might do that would make it less likely your drinker would do the behavior you just described or make the situation better.

I could first remind myself that his behavior does not reflect on me. Then I could take a deep breath and say to him, "I know you enjoy the drinks, but it is very important to me that you do not order another one tonight. Could you please do that for me?" If he insists on another, I will say, "If you choose to drink tonight, that's your business. However, I do not have to sit here and watch you. I'm going home now. When you sober up, I'd like to discuss this with you." Then I'll leave.

In this example you can see a few very important differences between the first and second responses. In the first, the partner lets Harris control the situation by losing her cool. Her response suggests that she accepts some responsibility for Harris's behavior. (Why else would his behavior embarrass her?) In comparison, the second response helps distance her from his behavior, which in turn helps her remain calm and avoid a confrontation. She begins by taking care of herself ("I'll remind myself that his behavior does not reflect on me") so that she can avoid blowing up and giving him an excuse to order a double. Then she acknowledges his feelings and expresses her own along with the request that he not order another drink. Failing that, she removes herself from the situation. The important points here are that her behavior was designed to give Harris every opportunity to change his pattern (without losing face) while protecting her own well-being. This may not always work exactly the way you want it to, but it does ensure that you don't buy into the negative pattern and that you do begin to set a new pattern.

As you think about how you can affect your loved one's behavior, keep these points in mind:

- If you become angry, you lose control of your behavior and the situation in general. In essence, you give control to the alcohol.
- Whenever possible, phrase your message in positive terms. That makes it more likely to be heard.
- While it is important to see each situation for what it is (the good, the bad, and the ugly), it is equally important not to catastrophize. In other words, focus on the here and now whenever you can. Don't turn tonight's debacle into a discussion of how your whole life is ruined. Seeing a catastrophe in every situation tends to trigger extreme emotions and loss of control.
- Progress happens each time you attempt to change the way you respond to a difficult situation. Whether your attempt is completely, partially, or not at all successful, having made the effort weakens the negative, unproductive habit pattern that you have practiced in the past. Progress comes

in many sizes and many forms. Take credit for every bit of it.

As you go forward, remind yourself daily that you can learn to change your behavior and your behavior can help your loved one to change. You do have the power.

Action Summary

The work you did in this chapter is comparable to turning the ignition key in your automobile. If you fail to activate the ignition, even the most finely tuned engines cannot operate. Similarly, if you do not believe you have the right and the power to take control of your life, you will not be able to use any tools we offer you. So remember that you are not the reason your loved one abuses alcohol or other drugs; each of us is responsible only for our own behavior. That said, keep in mind that you can change how you respond to your loved one and, in doing so, trigger positive changes in your lives.

Recap

• Refuse to take responsibility for anyone else's behavior. You are not the problem.
• Set your radar to watch for instances in which you could change your reaction to the drinker's behavior. As you work your way through the balance of this program, you will develop a number of tools to help you change the way you respond. The first step, though, is recognizing interactions in which you can apply them. Radar up!

Kathy and Jim: A New Kind of Love

Kathy knew what it was to feel responsible. She felt responsible for protecting the kids from Jim's drinking (both his behavior and his example). She felt responsible for smoothing things over for Jim at work when he'd wake up too sick to go in (after all, someone had to ensure they kept a roof over their heads). She felt responsible for protecting him from the scorn of family members and for protecting them from Jim's outbursts. She felt responsible for pushing him to drink with her nagging. She even felt responsible for feeling so miserable. And then something changed.

Kathy asked herself why it was all her responsibility. And there was no answer for the question. She still felt the children were her responsibility but everything else—well, she couldn't come up with a reason why it was her responsibility to make Jim look good or to clean up his messes. In particular, there was no reason to take the blame for his drinking. She never asked him to drink. She never "made" anyone else drink, and she had been close with other family members, friends, and old boyfriends. Other people in Jim's life were considerably less loving toward him than she was, and he never blamed them. There was simply no evidence for Jim's behavior being her fault.

Kathy decided that at least part of the reason she felt so responsible for Jim was because she loves him so much. Somehow, she figured, by taking responsibility for this terrifying turn in their lives, she must have been striving to fix it. When she finally accepted that the responsibility was not hers to take, two things happened. One was that she stopped beating herself up. She could take a breather. The second consequence was her head cleared, and she could think rationally about what she realistically *could* control. She figured out that her love for Jim could be the motivation to take care of herself so that she would have the energy to change the way she dealt with him. By doing that, Kathy pulled herself out of the endless loop of guilt/anger and started on a new road to a better life.

chapter 6

Let the Good Times Roll

Vanessa and Martin

By the time Vanessa turned twenty-one, she had already become an expert at taking care of her dad. Her mother passed away shortly after Vanessa's thirteenth birthday, and Martin, her father, never really recovered from the loss. At first he drank to "numb the pain," and then he drank "to forget." As time wore on, people came to expect him to be drunk and began avoiding him. Finally he seemed to drink just to fill the void where his life had once been. Through all of this, Vanessa was the one person who stood by him. In fact, she pretty much missed her adolescence while she raised her younger sister, argued with and cajoled her father in attempts to get him to quit, and devoted her time to running the household. Vanessa was old before her time and came into treatment feeling hopeless and resentful as well as guilty for feeling hopeless and resentful.

If you skimmed the table of contents before starting this book, chances are this chapter title caught your eye. What is a title like this doing in the middle of a serious book about a serious problem? Well, it's quite simple really. You deserve some fun.

Think of all the work and energy you have invested dealing

with problems caused by alcohol abuse. How many times have you pulled your family through a crisis or kept your loved one safe by hiding the car keys? Have you ever saved your kids from being verbally or physically abused? Have you taken on the role of father *and* mother or sole breadwinner? How much have you done to keep the delicate balance between a sane and insane life with a drinker? The answer is probably "a lot." In fact, we guess you have been working so hard at keeping your life together that you have given almost no time or attention to enjoying that life. It is time to change that.

Starting right now, begin rewarding yourself for your effort. In fact, reward yourself just for being you. As the title says, it's time to let the good times roll.

Self-reward (that's what we're talking about here) is not all that different from the kind of rewards you give family, friends, or co-workers. You smile at them, tell them they did a good job, or sometimes reward them with tangibles such as money, gifts, or special time. Rewarding ourselves only requires minor adjustments from the way we reward others. Instead of smiling at the outside world, you smile at yourself on the inside. Telling yourself that you've done well requires fewer resources than telling others; you don't need to say it out loud—just think it. You can reward yourself with physical things just as easily as you reward others—easier in fact because you don't have to guess at what would be a good reward. You know what you like.

Given that one of the major objectives of this program is to improve the quality of your life, it is essential that you introduce some good times into each day. No, you don't need to quit your job to make time for ball games and bubble baths. All you need to do is say something nice to yourself every day and plan a little time on most days for slightly bigger self-rewards. And don't worry if you haven't accomplished anything grand. Reward yourself just for having made it through the day. In fact, we'll go so far as to say *reward yourself for rewarding yourself!*

As we suggested above, self-reward comes in many forms. At its simplest and least expensive, it consists of positive self-talk, which means simply that you say nice things to yourself such as, "I am a dedicated person" or "I handled that situation better this time." Of course, your self-talk will vary depending on the situation. We call these Level 1 self-rewards. Slightly more complicated in terms of planning and expense are Level 2 rewards. They are free or inexpensive but do require time. Examples would be time off chores with a good novel; a long, hot soak in the tub; a bicycle ride through the park; or whatever activity brings you pleasure. Level 3 self-rewards are those we typically save for "Accomplishments" with a capital "A." For example, you might reward yourself with a professional massage (involves both time and money) after you successfully avoid losing your temper when your partner comes home drunk long after dinner has turned to charcoal.

Shortly, we will give you an activity in which you can develop your self-reward options and do some planning to make them a part of your life. First, though, we need to talk about how much to include or exclude your drinking loved one from your self-reward system.

To Roll with the Drinker, or Not

If your drinker is your spouse or life partner, there may be powerful forces acting on you to include him in your self-rewards. After all, the person you love is usually the one with whom you want to spend time. However, before you decide to reward yourself for all your hard work by going out to dinner with your loved one, give some thought to what this person will add to that activity. If she is likely to miss the dinner, show up drunk, or ruin the evening in some other way, your self-reward may well turn into a punishment. (If this describes your situation, take heart. Part of good therapy for substance abuse is working with the significant others of the abuser to improve their joint lives. Thus, if and when your loved one enters treatment, that process should help to make him a more enjoyable partner, and at that point you will derive pleasure from including him in your plans.)

On the other hand, including your drinker in your good times can also serve as a way of moving her away from a drinking lifestyle. By including her in activities that cannot be done while drinking (these are called "competing activities") and that are enjoyable to the two of you, you will limit the time available for drinking while maximizing the pleasurable time you spend together. Thus, it can be good for you, your loved one, and your relationship.

Having examined both sides of the coin, you are the one who must determine how much to involve your loved one in your self-rewards. Without knowing you personally, our generic recommendation is to plan most of your self-rewards around yourself and reliable friends and family and to include your drinker only in a limited fashion. As his behavior improves and becomes more reliable, you will be able to increase his involvement. In the meantime, though, don't let the drinker steamroll your good times.

Start Rolling

Take a few minutes now to begin adding some good times into your life. Use Activity 14 to start planning for more pleasure in your days. The activity has three columns, one for each level of self-reward we discussed earlier. Remember, Level 1 self-rewards are objects or activities that are free and/or instantaneous. Examples would include positive self-talk (the cheapest, most portable, and most powerful self-reward), a moment to sit by a warm fire, or playing favorite music while you do chores. Level 2 self-rewards involve some time and/or expense. Examples might include time to read a novel or a long-distance call to a friend. Level 3 includes all the other things that require more than a few minutes and more than a few dollars. Depending on your tastes (and budget), these may range from dinner out to a Caribbean cruise.

Read Vanessa's completed list below, then think about what you like to do and the way you like to think about yourself and in your notebook list as many things as you can in each category.

Activity 14. Good Times for Me

Level 1 Self-rewards (free, instant)	Level 2 Self-rewards (time, low-cost)	Level 3 Self-rewards (time, money)
Tell myself, "I can do it"	*Buy makeup*	*Buy myself flowers*
Say a prayer	*Call a friend*	*Treat myself to new shoes*
Smile at my reflection in the mirror	*Go to a meeting*	*Join a gym*
	Read a romance novel for a half hour	*Go to the gym*

Get By with a Little Help from Your Friends

People in distress tend to stay away from the people who are most likely to help and support them. Instead of letting friends and family lend a hand, they pull away from those who care about them and try to do it all alone. Although there is no research to tell us exactly why, experience says it is partly embarrassment, partly guilt, and partly shame. All of these are very real feelings and very common to people living with a problem drinker. However, isolating is counterproductive and unnecessary. Decide right now to put aside the feelings and thoughts that keep you locked away from your supporters and to embrace the message of the old Beatles song: "You can get by with a little help from your friends." Here's how.

First off, think about the people in your circle of family, friends, and acquaintances. Among all those individuals are some to whom you feel closer, some who are more fun to be with, and some who rank as the last people on earth with whom you want to spend any time. Start by crossing the last group off your list of potential supporters. Now you are left with a list of people who can fill various needs in your life.

Most of the people on your list are probably folks you would enjoy spending time with on a casual basis, just to have some fun. A few, however, will likely be individuals with whom you may want to talk about your situation. You will need two different approaches for each group of people. Let's talk first about how you can increase your contact with the first group—casual friends.

Create a Social Circle

If you have pretty much kept to yourself because of your loved one's drinking, it can be difficult to reenter the social world. Remember, however, that the difficulty is all inside your head. When you invite someone to go to a movie or meet for lunch, your discomfort comes from your concerns about how the person will react; perhaps the person will think you forward or desperate or foolish or who knows what. However, if you put the shoe on the other foot and imagine someone inviting you to get together, what would you think? Chances are you would be flattered, think the individual likes you, and generally be pleased. Why believe that other people would judge an invitation more harshly than you would? Even if the person has to turn you down, no harm is done, and odds are a new contact will have been established as the two of you agree to try some other time. The more people you attempt to connect with, the more likely you will be to find some new friends and increase the pleasure in your life.

Find a Confidante

Approaching individuals with whom you want to share your burden can be a little more difficult. However, it can be done. Here's how.

First, identify your goal. Do you want this person to just listen, give advice, physically protect you, loan money, or whisk you off to a desert island? Be very clear in your mind about what you are asking for. Keep your goal simple and focused. For example, reasonable goals would be: "I want someone to talk to about my frustrations with my wife's drinking problem. I don't want to feel judged or devalued."

Once you have a goal, figure out who the right person is to approach. Whom can you trust, who is a good enough friend? Decide whom you will ask to share your confidences.

Next, decide *how* you will ask. What words will you use? Our suggestion is the straightforward approach. Rather than beating around the bush or hinting at what you need, just say it. For example, "Dale, you and I have been friends for years, and you know that Gina's drinking is a problem. I wanted to know if we can find some time to talk so I can figure out what's going on with my life. I just need you to listen and support me. Would you do that for me?" Notice that this person was very direct and very specific about what he wanted from Dale.

Having chosen the words, there are only two more steps. The next, if you are nervous about asking for help, is to practice speaking the words. You can practice by imagining yourself speaking to the individual or by actually rehearsing the words out loud. The mirror makes a handy "partner" for practicing little speeches like this. However you do it, the point is to get your nervousness to a low enough level so that you are able to *do it*.

This brings us to the final step. Do it! Problems are difficult to tackle alone. Everyone needs a helping hand occasionally, and we all can get by with a little help from our friends.

If you are not confident in your ability to speak effectively in delicate situations, use Activity 15 to identify someone you would like to confide in and write down the words you will use to ask for this person's support. Having a written plan makes the task easier. Below you can see how Vanessa decided to ask for support from a girlfriend she's known all her life. Complete your own activity in your notebook.

◆ Activity 15. Ask for Help

Who will you ask for support?
Erica — we've been friends since kindergarten and she lives close by so it will be easy to get together.

Repeat the following statements to yourself:
1. There is nothing wrong with asking people for help. Everybody needs help at one time or another.
2. The problems we are having are not my fault. While I can help make things better or worse, I am not the one whose drinking is destroying our lives. I am working on the solution to our problems.
3. Helping others makes people feel good about themselves, so it is okay to ask this person for help.

Script your request. Tell the person what the problem is and be very clear in what you ask for.

Erica, I really need to talk to you about a problem. We've been friends our whole lives, and I know I can trust you. Before you say anything, I just want you to listen to me for two minutes. I need for you to be my friend, in confidence.

You know that I've been spending a lot of my time at home taking care of my dad. Well, Dad's problem is worse than you probably realize. And it keeps getting more and more out of control, and I just don't know

what to do. I need someone to talk to who won't judge me or give me
a hard time. I love you and need you to support me. Can I count on you
to help me through this?

---◆

When we talk to clients about self-reward and asking friends and family for help, they always agree wholeheartedly that these are terrific ideas and that they should definitely do them. At the end of the session, they leave with the intention of following our advice—and then something happens and they do not follow through. The next week when we ask how it went, they tell us that "life" got in the way and that they had time neither for self-reward nor connecting with friends. We say that is a lousy excuse. It wasn't life that got in the way. It was lack of planning. Life is always there, whether you are trying to find time to exercise or call a friend or take a nap. You *plan* time for and *make* time for the things that are important to you. Don't let your good times roll into a corner of your schedule and get covered with dust. If you really want to put pleasure and support back into your life, pull out your calendar right now and block off the time to complete this chapter's activities. Schedule your Level 1, 2, and 3 rewards as well as when you are going to call the people who will help you get by and get on with the good times.

Action Summary

Taking care of others begins with taking care of yourself. Begin working on putting your social life back together. Ask for company. Ask for help. Be nice to yourself.

Recap

• Plan Level 1, 2, and 3 rewards for yourself and make them happen.

- Implement an action plan to include other people in your life.

Kathy and Jim: The Pleasure Palace

When Kathy and Jim began dating, one of their favorite places to go on Friday nights was a combination restaurant/ dance hall called the Pleasure Palace. For about ten dollars, they could eat greasy burgers and fries and dance until their feet ached. When Kathy first started thinking about adding some fun to her own life, she found herself thinking more and more about the Pleasure Palace and started calling this part of the program her reconstruction project—because she was rebuilding the Pleasure Palace.

The first step in Kathy's reconstruction project was to make a list of compliments she felt she deserved and to promise herself to stop at the mirror every time she used the bathroom and compliment herself. She told herself, "I'm a good mother . . . a loyal wife . . . caring . . . organized . . . attractive . . . I have a future."

Kathy also wrote out a schedule for getting herself a manicure and pedicure every month (Level 2) and enrolled in an evening college class in Romantic literature (Level 3). In addition, Kathy decided it was high time to take her sister into her confidence about everything that was going on and admit that she sure could use some help. So she carefully thought through how she would ask her sister to listen to her and help her but not criticize Jim. (Kathy knew that old habits die hard, and if her sister said anything bad about Jim, she'd jump to his defense and end up arguing with her sister.)

Kathy made very specific plans, right down to what she

would say and when she would say it, and she stuck to them. The effect the bathroom mirror compliments had on Kathy surprised her. Kathy found herself coming out of the bathroom every few hours feeling just a little better about herself and a little more confident in her ability to accomplish her goals. She hadn't imagined that something so easy could have such a big effect.

When Kathy called her sister asking her to meet to talk about something important, Kathy's sister's heart skipped a beat. She didn't know whether it meant that Jim had beat up Kathy again (her sister knew about the first time even though Kathy thought she had hidden it) or whether, hope against hope, Kathy was going to leave him. Kathy was very clear with her sister about the kind of help she needed, and her sister promised to support her the way she asked. At the end of the evening, Kathy felt a load lift from her shoulders. She would get by with a little help and with the reconstruction of the Pleasure Palace.

chapter 7

Disable the Enabling

Vanya and Juan

Vanya and Juan had only been together a short time when Vanya began to think she had made a terrible mistake. They met at church. He was attracted to her vivaciousness and quick wit. She found him handsome and was excited by his rough-and-ready nature. Juan had never graduated from high school, and he worked for a construction company. He was hard-working and hard-playing—unlike most of the men Vanya had dated in the past. What he lacked in finesse, she said, he more than made up for in masculinity. There was something raw and vital about him that captured her imagination, and then her heart. At first, life together was thrilling . . . and then the thrills turned into something considerably less exciting. Juan's drinking increased and so did the negative consequences.

Don't Be the Fixer

As the healthier partner in your relationship, it has naturally fallen on you to keep things together and pick up the pieces as they fall. It is common for people in your position to ignore their needs in order to "take care" of the drinker and the

109

family. Unfortunately, by being so helpful, you also accomplish two very *un*helpful things. One is that you save others' lives at the expense of draining your own. Each time you ignore your needs to take care of others, you use up a little more of your energy reserves. Eventually, you will be so used up that you will either collapse (physically, mentally, or motivationally), or you will continue to try to help but your efforts will become less and less effective. You will be running on empty.

The other consequence of fixing is that you make it easy for the drinker to continue in her present behavior pattern. As long as you are there to clean up the mess, square things with the boss, and generally fix what breaks, there is no need for the drinker to change. The popular term to describe this pattern of the drinker drinking and you picking up the pieces is "enabling." By always being there to fix what goes wrong, you show him that you accept the drinking. Your words may be to the contrary as you scold, nag, and instruct—but your behavior shouts, "I'm here to make it easier for you!"

The more you give, the more the drinker takes until your life is no longer your own. Everything you do centers on either avoiding bad consequences of your drinker's behavior, cleaning up the mess, or feeling hurt and angry that you are caught in this trap. What starts out as good intentions to help your drinker turns into relationship poison as it makes drinking easier for your loved one and leaves you feeling used and angry.

To illustrate, consider Juan and Vanya. Juan is a heavy drinker and has lost several jobs because of it. His typical pattern is to control his intake enough during the week to not cause problems but to get plastered on the weekend and then not be able to go to work on Monday morning. After several "no shows" and calling in sick, he is fired. This has been going on for years, and Vanya is worried Juan will lose the job he just recently started. Juan does fine the first two weeks and then, true to form, gets together with his buddies to watch football on Sunday and ties one on. Monday morning Vanya cannot get him out of bed, and he tells her to call his boss and say he's sick. Thinking only about saving his job, which the family desperately needs, Vanya makes the call. On the surface, this is what any loving partner would do, isn't it? Of course. But if you look a little more carefully, you will see that Vanya is sending an unspoken message to Juan. She's telling him that he can drink as much as he wants and she, through her actions, agrees to be responsible for his behavior. Juan can drink without cost.

Anyone can be an enabler. See if you can identify the enabling behaviors in the following examples. These behaviors come up a lot in our practice.

> Alan is in his early twenties. His friends describe him as "the original party animal," and he takes great pride in living up to the label. Most nights he stays out all night drinking and then sleeps until well past noon during the day. Needless to say, he has not had any success at holding a job and as a result still lives with his parents. Alan's parents are naturally distraught by his behavior but love him and do what they can to help. They do not nag him about his habits nor require him to pay rent or contribute to the household in any way. They believe that if they provide a safe, accepting environment for him, Alan will eventually grow up and come to his senses.

> George is so worried about the possibility that his wife will crash her car coming home from a bar that he makes a point of always having her favorite liquor on hand so she will not stop for a drink on the way home

from work. "After all," he says, "she is going to drink anyway, so it's better she does it at home where she can't kill herself in a car wreck."

Alicia was sixteen when she got her first DUI. Coming home from a Friday night football game at the high school, she was pulled over for driving too slowly, and she failed the field sobriety test. When the police notified her parents, they rushed down to the station, paid her bail, got her car out of impound, and took her home where she was tucked safely into bed. From there, they hired an expensive attorney who was able to have the charges dismissed. Feeling they had saved their daughter from significant trauma, Alicia's parents made her promise not to drink again but did not take away her car because she "needed" it to get to school.

Alan's parents, Alicia's parents, George, and Vanya all mean well, but all are guilty of fixing, or enabling. Through love and ignorance they are making it easier for their loved ones to drink with impunity. Juan never has to drag his aching body out of bed or face his boss with his excuses. Alicia has learned that she can even get away with breaking the law and Mommy and Daddy will make everything all right; there is no reason for her to change. Alan doesn't have to do anything. He pleases himself and everything else is taken care of by his parents. As long as they do not require any changes from him in exchange for their support, they are guaranteed no changes. George is also enabling his wife's drinking by making it easy for her to indulge. She doesn't need to think about when or where to drink, what the possible consequences are, or face the fact that her drinking is breaking her husband's heart. For all of these drinkers, there are no costs. They have as close to a free ride as anybody comes.

The hardest thing to do to someone you love is to let her experience the natural consequences of her behavior. But, if you really love the person, you must. Think about what fixing behaviors you do that might be enabling your drinker and think about what consequences it is time he experienced. Activity 16 will help you jot down your thoughts. As you can see from the example, Mark (from chapter 4) realized that much of what he did for Maria to motivate her to change actually had the opposite effect, making it easier for her to continue drinking. Complete the activity in your notebook.

Activity 16. Fixing Behaviors

How do you make it easier for your loved one to drink than it would be if he or she did not have you, or anyone like you, around?

Buy booze, clean up, make excuses when she can't keep appointments, tell her it's not her fault, give her rides when she loses her keys or license, let her lies slide because I'm too sad to question them, carry her to bed when she's too sloshed to walk

Old Habits Die Hard

As you move toward your goals and away from your fixing/enabling pattern, you will vividly experience the truth of this heading: Old habits die hard . . . *very hard*. You and your drinker have been interacting the same way for so long that the two of you have really perfected the dance. You can push each other's buttons without so much as lifting a mental finger. Moreover, familiar is always more comfortable than new (at least in the emotional arena), so even change for the better is initially uncomfortable. Your drinker will react to the change, and you will find *yourself* resisting it as well—even though it's your own doing.

We have seen it time and again. Someone comes into treatment because life with the drinker has become unbearable and any kind of change seems like a blessing. Then, the relationship really does start to change and the very same person who arrived at the clinic in desperate search of relief from her present situation gets cold feet.

"I love him. He's such a good man. It's the liquor that's bad."

"She's my child, I can't abandon her."

"We've been together for seventeen years, I can't change the rules on him now."

"What happens if I try to change and she leaves me?"

"He's my dad. I owe him."

"If I don't cover up, what would people think about us?"

We've heard thousands of reasons to let things remain unchanged once people are faced with the natural discomfort of the unfamiliar. The truth, however, is that the feelings people have when they first decide to make a change (like when you first began this book) are the real feelings. Your frustration, anger, depression, and longing for change are still real. When you find yourself thinking, "Things aren't that bad," chances are you are just reacting to the stress of change. It's tough, but if you recognize what you are doing and keep your eye on your goal, you can move forward. Nothing magically changes. Your drinker will not wake up tomorrow a new person, and you will not be able to help her by doing what you have been doing for years. It hasn't worked.

Habits That Don't Work

You and your drinker are unique, but some habits are so common it is a safe bet you will recognize at least a few of the following as your own.

Fixing

You "fix" what your drinker breaks. Day after day you pick up the pieces. Your drinker wakes up too hungover to go to work, so you call her boss and "explain." Or he comes home drunk, vomits all over the bathroom floor, and you clean up the mess. The phone rings at 2:00 A.M. and your drinker has (fortunately) forgotten where she left the car and needs you to come pick her up—so you do.

From where you are sitting, it may seem like fixing is the humane or sensible thing to do. After all, no one would let someone they love sleep in vomit or on a street corner. We agree. If you consider the short-term consequences, it would be inhumane to do that. However, think about the long-term consequences. Each time you fix the situation, your drinker has one more powerful learning experience. What does he learn? The drinker learns that no matter how irresponsibly he behaves, there are no consequences! You will take care of everything. Sure, he may have to listen to you complain the next day . . . but what's a little nagging when you get what you want without having to pay for it?

Instead of Fixing

If you want your drinker to change her lifestyle, you absolutely have to let her be responsible for it. If she comes home plastered and deposits dinner and cocktails all over her dress, let her sleep in it. There will be a more constructive lesson learned in the morning when she awakens to the stink of last night than if you clean it all up and tuck her in for sweet dreams. Similarly, anyone old enough to earn a hangover on a weeknight is old enough to call the boss himself the next morning. If your drinker becomes belligerent and tells off her parents, let her be the one to apologize and make things right again. Stop providing a free ride. It's not easy (you also have to face the stink of last night), but in the long run it will pay off.

Nagging

We thought about calling this habit "instructing" or "teaching" because "nagging" has such a nasty feel to it, and your intention is anything but nasty. But let's be honest. From where the drinker sits, your well-intentioned comments are just plain old nagging.

For instance, your drinker comes home drunk, and you remind him about the terrible impact his drinking has on your life together. You are upset, concerned, and have the right to express those feelings. However, he shrugs it off and goes to sleep. This pattern goes on for years. He comes in late. You nag.

What actually may be happening is that you are reinforcing (rewarding) him for coming home late and drunk. A fact of human nature is that we do not waste much energy on behaviors that have no payoff. If someone does the same thing over and over, you can bet there is something rewarding about the situation.

A trained eye may see the obvious; your lecturing must not bother him much since he continues the behavior month after month. In fact, he may enjoy the attention or enjoy the fact that he has you at his beck and call. Even though you feel you are choosing to wait up and lecture him, it is his behavior that causes you to do so. There may be a power play going on here.

The drinker may also feel a weird sort of endorsement by you because you are there waiting for him. Think about it. There may be some comfort in knowing that no matter how much he drinks or how late he stays out, you will be there singing your usual song when he comes home. So the lesson for the drinker is that drinking doesn't take away any of the comforts of home. It's a free ride.

Instead of Nagging

Try using an "I feel" statement to let your drinker know she has hurt you, but without attacking. First, though, think about what you want your words to achieve. Do you just want to make sure your drinker knows he has hurt you? If so, say so and enjoy the resulting argument. If, on the other hand, you are trying to get your drinker to behave differently, keep that goal in mind and use your words to let her know what behavior is hurting you now.

For instance, remember in chapter 5 when Mom was nagging John about coming home late from school again because he stopped to drink with the boys? Our guess is her goal was to get John home safely and in time to eat with the family, but every time she nagged John, he would either leave to drink more or become angry and mean. It's definitely time to try something different. Instead of getting into it with John, Mom could use an "I feel" statement. She might say, "I feel bad when I know you're out drinking" or "I miss you when you're not home to eat with the family" and leave it at that. Later, when John is sober and she senses he is in a good mood, Mom can approach him and tell him as positively as possible what she would like to see in the future and what she will do if it does not happen. For instance, she may say, "I worry about you when you come home late, but from now on I'm not going to sit and wait for you. I'm going to do something for myself. So if you are late and I'm not home, don't worry. It only means I've gone to visit my mother, or I've gone to an Al-Anon meeting."

Protecting

Although protecting the ones you love sounds like a good idea, it may not be. Just like fixing and nagging, protecting can have both a positive and a negative effect. Sometimes by protecting people, you keep them from learning how to protect themselves.

Consider the wife who repeatedly calls her husband's work to say he is sick. Every time she covers up for him, she supports his drinking. He gets to drink without facing any consequences. He does not have to drag himself in to work feeling lousy. He does not have to bear the discomfort of lying to his supervisor. He doesn't even have to awaken early to make the call. He does not have to suffer the repercussions of not showing up to work without having called in sick. All he has to do is continue drinking as much as he likes, comfortable that his wife will pay the piper. He gets a heck of a good deal.

Science and experience both tell us that if the drinker is not required to take responsibility for the negative consequences of her drinking, unwanted behavior is not likely to change. Indeed, the typical course of events is for things to become progressively worse. If you want them to improve, if you really want to help your drinker, you must stop protecting him.

People tell us so often that they buy liquor for their drinker in an effort to keep her home and safe. The rationale goes like this, "If I buy her favorite liquor, she'll come home to drink and won't be in a position to get in a car wreck or receive a DWI." A variation on this is, "If I call in sick for him when he's hungover, he won't be as likely to get fired, and our life won't go down the tubes." It sounds terribly reasonable, but is it?

To begin with, buying liquor for a drinker is giving her permission to drink. If you give permission to drink at home, it is a short step to seeing that as permission to drink everywhere. Further, what happens if she comes home and drinks for an hour or two and *then* decides to go to a bar? Your efforts will have totally backfired. Although you feel as if you are protecting your drinker, this behavior actually fuels the problem.

Instead of Protecting

A more constructive way to "help" would be to make a list of nondrinking activities he enjoys, especially those that are difficult to do while drinking, and engage your loved one in one of those at the time he would normally drink. You might also consider stocking up on his favorite nonalcoholic beverages and first-choice foods to provide an alternative to liquor.

Take the quiz below to see if you are a "protector." Read each statement and in the space provided write down how many times you have done that action in the past six months. For instance, if you have brought liquor home three times during the past six months, place a 3 beside that action.

Number
of Times   Protective Action

_____   Picked up your drinker from a bar in the middle of the night

_____   Called your drinker's boss to "explain" an absence

_____   Paid an overdue bar bill to prevent the owner from taking action against your drinker

_____   Made excuses to family members for your drinker's failure to show up at family get-togethers

_____   Made excuses to friends for your drinker's failure to show up at planned get-togethers

_____   Made excuses to family members for your drinker's behavior when he or she has gotten drunk and unpleasant

_____   Made excuses to friends for your drinker's behavior when he or she has gotten drunk and unpleasant

_____   Brought liquor home so your drinker would not go out to drink

_____   Refused to make plans with family members because you did not want to risk exposing your drinker to them during a particularly bad period

_____   Refused to make plans with friends because you did not want to risk exposing your drinker to them

_____ Told stories about others who drink more than
your drinker

_____ Bailed your drinker out of jail

_____ Helped your drinker look for items lost while
drinking

_____ Laundered his or her soiled clothing

_____ Acted like a nurse when he or she was drunk

_____ Nursed your drinker's alcohol-related injuries

_____ Hid problems from family and children

_____ Persuaded family members not to discuss the
drinking problems

_____ Been your drinker's alarm clock and made sure he
or she got to work on time

_____ Made specific foods to help mend a hangover

_____ Told your drinker that his or her inappropriate
behavior wasn't that bad

_____ Consoled your drinker when he or she felt guilt or
remorse

_____ Downplayed the seriousness of your drinker's
behavior

_____ Cut back your own spending because your drinker
spent too much on drinking

Figure out your score by adding together all your answers.
If you score more than zero, it is time for you to start pulling
back and letting your drinker pay his or her own way. Any
score more than zero tells us you are punishing yourself for
your drinker's behavior—a losing strategy. You pay, and he or
she learns it's okay. It is **not** okay!

Out with the Old

Now that you see how your old behaviors may actually have
supported drinking, let's look at why past efforts to get your
loved one to stop have failed. You don't want to dwell on

failed attempts, but you do need to clear out the old to make room for the new. To do that, think about the strategies you have used over the years to get your drinker to quit. Stimulate your memory by looking at the examples below. Check off each strategy you have tried and add any that we have missed.

Did you ever . . .

_____ Ask him or her to stop drinking or to drink less?

_____ Hide liquor or throw it out?

_____ Give your drinker printed information on AA or other ways to stop drinking?

_____ Encourage him or her to see a spiritual advisor?

_____ Leave your drinker temporarily?

_____ Hide his or her wallet, checkbook, or money?

_____ Ask friends or employers to intervene?

_____ Get drunk yourself, to show your drinker what it's like?

_____ Threaten to get a divorce?

_____ Threaten to take the children away?

_____ Cover up for his or her mistakes caused by drinking and let your drinker feel guilty for it?

_____ Avoid friends and family due to drinking problems and let your drinker feel guilty?

_____ Have arguments over his or her drinking?

_____ Let your drinker know he or she has lost your trust and respect?

_____ Accuse your drinker of embarrassing you in public?

_____ Call the police or 911 to stop his or her drinking?

_____ Take on the job of searching the car and home for alcohol?

_____ Reason with your drinker about the pros and cons of drinking?

_____ Plead with your drinker to stop?

_____ (Fill in other tactics you may have tried that we've missed here.)

If you have repeatedly done any of these and your loved one is still drinking, it is a safe bet these strategies do not work. So review them, study them, and throw them away. Get rid of those failed strategies and replace them with something that will be more productive. What do you have to lose? If it doesn't work, you won't be any worse off than before you began, and our experience tells us that more than 75 percent of the people who use this strategy have results that satisfy them. There's no reason to think you won't too.

In with the New

All those unsatisfactory tactics you have used in the past are about to be replaced by powerful new techniques. The enjoyable activities you listed in chapter 6 will slowly but surely replace the negative ones, such as avoiding friends because of embarrassment and staying home to keep an eye on your drinker. The next three chapters (8, 9, and 10) give you the nuts and bolts to replace enabling behaviors with constructive ones.

Action Summary

Review your interactions with your drinker and look for what you might be doing that enables your drinker to continue drinking. Keep an eye out for fixing, nagging, and protecting.

Recap

• Fixing the messes made by your loved one because of abuse only makes it that much easier for her to continue making the same mistakes over and over. Allowing her to experience the real-life consequences of her behavior is more likely to result in positive change.

- Rather than wasting your energy nagging and reminding your loved one about the negative consequences of drinking and drugging, calmly tell him how you feel about what is going on and then withdraw your attention.
- Sometimes by trying to protect someone, we actually hurt this person. Make sure that your efforts to keep your loved one safe are constructive, such as engaging her in enjoyable nondrinking activities, rather than destructive, such as keeping liquor in the house in an attempt to prevent her from driving while impaired.

Kathy and Jim: Pay the Piper

The concept of enabling blew Kathy out of the water when she first heard about it. "Do you mean I've been messing it up all these years?" she cried. "I was trying to help, not make it easier for him to drink!"

Kathy soon calmed down and understood that she wasn't doing anything "bad." She was merely doing what felt right to her, even though the results were not what she intended. But she was now committed to making effective, productive changes, and so she reviewed her typical responses to Jim's drinking and identified a number of enabling behaviors that she targeted for change.

Although there were quite a number of things Kathy decided to change, the most important one to her was her habit of protecting Jim from disappointing the kids. In the past, whenever he would come home in one of "those" moods, Kathy would quickly find something for the children to do outside or in their rooms so they wouldn't see Daddy stumbling or slurring his words. She knew how important it was for Jim to be respected by his children and went to great lengths to keep him from looking bad in front of them. But no more.

The next time Jim came stumbling into the house, Kathy did not hustle the kids out of sight. They saw Daddy stumble through the door and miss the closet bar when he went to hang up his coat. Jim tried to talk nice to the kids but his words came out slurred, and he saw the children pull back. They were frightened, and it showed. Jim tried again to ask them about their day, but the youngest girl started crying and ran to hide her face in Kathy's skirt. Jim just stood there for a moment. Then he said, "Shit," and went into the bedroom. Kathy heard him shower and get into bed.

Something changed that evening.

chapter 8

Problem Solving

Richard and Louise

Richard and Louise had been married for seven years when she started coming home from work every night and fixing herself a drink. "I need it to unwind," she said. At first Richard didn't think much of it, but as time went on, Louise went from one to two or three drinks each evening and eventually got into the habit of skipping dinner, drinking all evening, and falling asleep in the recliner.

Richard tried everything he knew of to make Louise cut down. He scolded her, making her feel guilty and useless. He pleaded with her, appealing to her sense of family duty. He raged at her, often threatening to leave her or throw her out on the street. Nothing worked.

Finally, Richard decided to look at the old problem in a different light. . . .

Old Problems in a New Light

As you travel the road of change, you face the challenge of figuring out new ways to handle situations you have handled a thousand times in the past—but in ways that did not work very well. The problem-solving strategy we teach is designed to help you design solutions that work. By following the steps outlined here, you will be able to generate a number of possible solutions and make the best decisions about which to use.

Step 1: Define the Problem

The key to problem solving is coming up with a really specific description of the problem. The more specifically and completely you can describe what needs to change, the easier it will be to change it. For example, when Richard vaguely described the problem he was having with Louise as "she drinks too much and ruins our time together," he had a difficult time coming up with strategies for changing his situation. He tried talking to her, yelling at her, crying, ignoring the problem—but somehow he always felt like he was wearing scuba diving gear while skydiving. When he finally sat down and asked himself exactly what situations and behaviors made up her "drinking too much," he was able to break the big mess he felt their life was into smaller, more manageable problems. In this case he could define the problem as Louise's pattern of responding to a stressful day at work by overdrinking. When Richard looked at it this way, he could see that her response to stress provided a good starting place for him. So he defined the problem as having to come up with a new way to lessen the effects of work stress and to help her unwind without drinking.

Step 2: Brainstorm

The best way to come up with new ideas is to turn off your internal editor. In other words, make a list of every possible solution you can think of—*regardless of whether it makes sense, is realistic, or is absolutely ridiculous*. Richard's list of all the possible (realistic and ridiculous) ways he could help Louise unwind without overdrinking is shown below. As you can see, he was able to turn off that internal voice we call our editor; you know, the voice that says, "That's a dumb idea" or "It'll never work." Once Richard had as long a list as he could think of, he moved on to Step 3.

Richard's brainstorming list of possible ways to help Louise unwind			
• Tell her to chill	• Limit her to one drink	• Call her selfish	• Make her feel guilty
• Offer her tea	• Offer to fix dinner	• Remind her everyone has rough days	• Play a relaxation tape
• Get rid of the kids	• Draw her a bath	• Plan a vacation	• Have wild sex
• Rub her neck	• Give her a massage	• Give her a shampoo	• Play soothing music
• Rent her favorite movie	• Sing to her	• Throw a tantrum	• Walk in the park
	• Dance with her		• Feed her ice cream

Step 3: Evaluate and Select a Solution

When your list is as long as you can possibly make it and your internal editor has been as quiet as you can make it, it is time to sort through your ideas. Some of them will obviously be unrealistic and you can cross them off right away. Now go through the rest of the list and rate each idea for how likely you think it is to work and for how easy it is to do. Above all, if the activity is supposed to compete with drinking, remember it must be rewarding to your drinker. Also, don't just pick your favorite idea and ignore the rest. You might find out the favorite one doesn't work and that you need a backup. Rate them all, and then circle the one that you rated as the most likely to succeed and as easy to do. This is your first choice for a solution to your problem. This is your plan.

You can see what Richard did with his brainstorming list in Step 3. Happily, he decided that getting rid of the kids was not an option. He also eliminated a few other ideas that did not feel realistic. As you can see, he concluded that a neck rub and an offer to fix dinner while she bathed were his two top choices.

Richard's evaluation and selection

Rejects	Possibilities	How likely?	How easy?
Tell her to chill	*Offer to fix dinner*	*Very*	*Very*
Get rid of the kids	Draw her a bath	Very	Somewhat
Throw a tantrum	Give her a massage	Very	Somewhat
	Sing to her	Not!	Very
Make her feel guilty	Offer her tea	Somewhat	Very
Remind her everyone has	Rent her favorite movie	Somewhat	Not convenient
rough days	*Rub her neck*	*Very*	*Very*
	Plan a vacation	Somewhat	Somewhat
Call her selfish	Give her a		
Have wild sex	shampoo	No idea!	Not convenient
Walk in the park	Play soothing		
Limit her to one drink	music	Somewhat	Very
	Feed her ice		
Play a relaxation tape	cream	Somewhat	Very
Dance with her			

Step 4: Try It and Track It

Once you have a plan of action, try it. But don't do what you've done all these years—trying and trying and trying. This time, try like a scientist. That means implement your plan and keep track of how it works. It is best to actually write out how you will handle the problem the next time it occurs and then make notes as soon as possible after you try it. This way, you will be able to tell exactly how well it worked or, if it fell short, just what parts need adjustment. Sometimes you will be able to adjust your plan just a little to make it right. Other times you will need to go back to Step 3 and select a new solution.

At the end of Step 3, Richard wrote out his plan for the next time Louise came home from work in a nasty mood. Below you can see his notes about how his plan went the first few times he tried it.

Plan: When Louise comes home griping about her boss, I will rub her neck and tell her how much the kids and I appreciate her. Then I'll suggest she take a hot bath while I fix dinner.

Oct. 5: She came home in one of those moods, and I rubbed her neck and said nice stuff to her. But I really wanted to be together, so I suggested we fix dinner together. It started out okay until the kids got into a screaming match and Louise's mood went down the drain. She ended up drunk and asleep on the sofa by the time I got done putting the kids to bed.

Plan revision: Stick with the darn plan next time and try it again!

Oct. 11: Another one of those days at work for her. This time I followed the neck rub and nice words with an offer to fix dinner while she bathed. Louise loved the idea and went off happily. About halfway through fixing dinner, I heard the children knocking on the bathroom door wanting to know when Mom was going to start working on Halloween costumes. Louise cut her bath short and came downstairs clearly annoyed. She insisted one drink with dinner would help calm her down but . . . the usual story.

Plan revision: Keep the kids out of her hair and calm.

Oct. 15: Here we go again. This time, I did everything as planned and made the kids stay in the kitchen with me.

Louise was able to soak in the tub and came down to dinner with a smile on her face. At one point during the evening she suggested we have a drink together, but I told her how much I was enjoying just our being together and she let the topic go. Success!

Step 5: Evaluate, Refine, or Try Another Idea

This step really happens pretty much together with Step 4. As you implement your plans and track them, you will have ideas for how to improve them. As you saw in Richard's notes, each time he described how the evening went, he also adjusted his plan to make it more effective.

Please remember, always, that the changes you are working on are changes in how you and your drinker *live*. By definition, they are dynamic, or ever changing. It will never be the case that you decide on a way of responding to a person or situation and never have to modify it. From day to day to month to year, we change. Our plans and approaches for interacting have to change too. Do not be discouraged if your plans do not work perfectly the first time or the fiftieth time. Just keep tracking and refining. It will come together for you.

Action Summary

If it hasn't worked in the past, it's unlikely to work now. If the problem is still there, examine it under a new light.

Recap

- Define the problem.
- Brainstorm solutions—lock your internal editor out of the room.
- Evaluate your solutions and select one to try.

- Try it and track it.
- Evaluate, refine, or try another idea.

Kathy and Jim: Finding New Paths

As Kathy gradually made changes in how she responded to Jim's drinking behavior, she began to feel pretty good about their future. He was still drinking more than was good for their relationship, but the physical violence had not happened in months and Jim's general mood around the house was considerably improved. There was still a fair bit of work left to be done before Kathy was willing to accept the situation as permanent. In particular, Kathy really wanted Jim to spend more time with the children, but whenever she suggested it and he agreed to take them bowling the upcoming Friday, he would sabotage the plans by having a couple of beers when he got home from work. Then Kathy would drop the idea of an outing because she didn't want him drinking and then driving with the children in the car.

Kathy decided that her gentle suggestions, angry reprimands, and tactical cajoling just weren't going to do the trick. So she decided to look at the problem in a new light. First, she tried to put her finger on the heart of the problem (that is, clearly define it). She knows that Jim loves their kids and wants to have a relationship with them. In looking over the pattern of aborted father-children outings, she identified what she thought was the real problem. She had always brought up the subject during the week, and Jim, wanting to be with his kids, would agree and plan it for the end of the week—Friday. The problem was that when he would get home from work at the end of the day, he would be tired and a little irritable. The kids, on the other hand, would be revved up and ready to go bowling with Dad. The resulting combination was a tired, irritable father and a roomful of noisy, rambunctious children—not a recipe for success. Kathy made a list of possible solutions, including rehearsing the children on appropriate behavior for when Dad came home and having them ready to leave the moment he walked into the house so there would be no time for beer. The best solution, she felt, was what she humorously called her one-two punch. She again suggested to Jim that he take the children bowling, but when he agreed to do so the following Friday, she told him that at the end of a tough work week she thought it would be better to drop the kids off at her parents and just the two of them go out for supper (her one punch). Then (the two punch), on Saturday afternoon, after he had slept in and lazed around the house for a while, bowling would be a fun outing, not only for the kids but for Jim as well. Jim thought this was a great idea and agreed to the plan.

When the weekend rolled around again, Jim and Kathy enjoyed their dinner out; he started to order a beer at dinner but caught the look of disappointment on Kathy's face and stopped himself. Everyone enjoyed the trip to the bowling alley Saturday afternoon—even Kathy who got a blessed afternoon of quiet at home as a result.

chapter 9

Communication

Harold and DeeAnne

"Every single time we try to talk about anything more personal than the football scores, we get into a major fight," DeeAnne told us when she called the clinic. "It seems as though he goes out of his way to do the things that make me mad. Even when I ask him really nicely to stop something or to do something for me, he starts yelling and uses it as an excuse to get another drink. He knows how much I hate it when he drinks that much!"

At the heart of every relationship is communication. If the people in the relationship cannot find a way to tell each other what they need, what they want, and what they appreciate in each other, the relationship is skating on thin ice.

Communicate

We talked a little about communication style in chapter 5 where we gave examples of how to translate your statements from negative to positive. For example, instead of saying, "I hate it when you drink," you could make the statement more positive by saying, "I love being with you when you're sober."

Both statements ask for the same result (sobriety) but one uses fighting words and the other uses loving words.

When relationships run into hard times, drinking-related or not, there are four predictable changes in the way partners communicate: They stop using statements that (1) are *Positive*, (2) begin with *I*, (3) show *Understanding*, and (4) demonstrate a willingness to *Share* responsibility for the situation. In other words, their communication patterns are no longer PIUS. As the relationship becomes more and more conflictual, conversations lose their positive components and focus almost exclusively on the negative. Participants tend to make "you" statements in place of "I" statements, and they stop letting the other person know that they understand how the other feels. Finally, they stop sharing responsibility for their life together and focus on trying to assign blame.

PIUS statements have a softer feel to them. The listener doesn't feel attacked and therefore is less likely to counterattack. It is not difficult to learn a more gentle communication style, but it does take practice. When you have been attacking each other for some time and have a history of hurt feelings, changing how you communicate is at first a little like swimming upstream; it is possible but you have to concentrate. What you will find, though, is that if you make the effort to improve the way you communicate, your drinker will find fewer excuses to respond negatively to you.

Positive Statements

Since we talked about using positive statements earlier, we will not repeat ourselves here. However, it is helpful to review examples of how negative statements can be turned into positive statements. Take the time to read the following list and think about some of the statements you have said to your loved one recently.

Negative	Positive
1. You always screw up the evening.	1. I enjoy you so much when you don't drink.
2. You make it impossible to keep track of our checking account.	2. Please help me keep the checking account straight by entering the checks you write into the registry.
3. You and your buddies made a mess of this place.	3. I'm glad your friends like coming here. Could you help me keep it tidy so it looks good for company?
4. You always embarrass me.	4. It would make me so happy if you drank soda tonight.
5. I'm not having sex with you when you're drunk.	5. I'd enjoy making love to you when you're sober.
6. I can't stand it when you lie to me.	6. I want to believe you but that story seems odd.
7. You never listen to me when I'm talking to you.	7. I understand that some of our discussions are upsetting, but I'd love it if you could help me work them out.
8. You SOB. You stole money out of my purse without asking. I'm going to kill you!	8. It's sad that you have to take money from me. I guess I'll have to keep my money in a safer place.
9. Don't ever let me catch you yelling at the kids like that again, you bully.	9. I know the kids can be frustrating, but please help me set a good example by talking to them calmly.
10. I can't stand you, you selfish jerk. You missed my parents' anniversary party on purpose.	10. Maybe it wasn't clear to you that my parents' thirtieth anniversary party was tonight. I sure wished you were there.
11. Why don't you get off your butt and find a job. You've been unemployed for six months. Don't you have any self-respect?	11. I know not working must be difficult for you. Is there anything I can do to help?

"I" Statements

The quickest way to elicit a fight is to make someone feel attacked. And the easiest way to do that is by beginning your statement with the word "you." As soon as most people hear this word, they prepare for attack—and for good reason. Beginning a sentence with "you" flags the listener that she is about to be the center of attention. Given the habitually conflictual nature of your relationship, your drinker naturally expects this focus to be an attack. Hence, she prepares for fight or flight. From there it is a quick breath to an argument.

When you talk to your drinker about problems or emotional issues, make it a point to tell him how you feel or what you want, not what he is doing wrong. The examples below will make this clear.

Sample "I" Statements

With the sting	Without the sting
1. You're so inconsiderate for missing dinner without calling.	1. I feel hurt when you miss dinner without calling.
2. You're an accident waiting to happen when you drink.	2. I get scared when you drink so much.
3. You shouldn't drink tonight.	3. I would be so happy if you did not drink this evening.
4. You're a slob.	4. It's important to me to have a tidy home. Won't you please put your things away?

Understanding Statements

There is another piece to the communication puzzle that will help the two of you get along better in spite of the problems you discuss. Try to include "understanding statements" in your discussions. That is, let your loved one know that you understand her and that you care about her feelings. For instance, let's say you are trying to get your drinker to go out and look for a job. You can use all the techniques we have already discussed and say, "Honey, I am so worried about our financial situation right now. It would really help if you sent out some job applications today." That would be a great start. However, it would be even better if you added an understanding statement to let your loved one know you appreciate how difficult this is for him. Thus, you might say, "Honey, I know how frustrating it is for you to job hunt in this tough market, but I'm so worried. . . ."

Showing that you understand how the other person feels makes it easier for that person to hear you without feeling she has to defend herself.

Share the Responsibility

We have spent a lot of time exploring how your behavior is intertwined with that of your drinker. Even though you are not the cause of the problem, you are intimately involved with it and do have an effect on it. Thus, it makes sense to share some of the responsibility for things that go wrong. (Not in all cases, but when appropriate.)

When you ask your drinker to make a change, along with acknowledging how difficult it is, let your loved one know that you see yourself as part of the picture. Keep in mind, however, that you do not need to take responsibility for everything that goes wrong or for your drinker's behavior. You just need to acknowledge that you are part of whatever situation is going on. Here are examples of how you might do this.

- "I understand that you get upset when the kids make so much noise. Maybe I could get them to play in their room so you can concentrate on looking at the want ads."

- "I know it's partly my fault that we argue so much. I'm going to try to be more understanding, and I hope you will also try to see my side of the issues."
- "I know I sometimes react strongly to your drinking even when it's uncalled for. Let's work together to solve our differences."

One of the easiest ways to show that you see yourself as part of the situation and to defuse an emotional situation is to say something along the lines of, "Can I help? You look upset."

PIUS Communication in Action

Now it is time to look at how DeeAnne softened her communication approach to Harold. Activities 17 and 18 walk you through the changes she made. As you review the examples, think about how you would apply the PIUS style to your life. Then work both activities in your notebook.

Activity 17. Past Arguments

Think about the last three arguments you had with your loved one that began with you trying to tell or ask him/her something. Describe each one in as much detail as you can.

Argument #1

Harold and I were going to meet some friends for dinner, and on the way there I asked him, "Please don't drink tonight because you always get drunk and embarrass me." He replied that he doesn't always get drunk and if I'm so embarrassed by him, why do I even go out with him. I yelled something back . . . can't remember what now . . . and we ended up turning around to go home.

Argument #2

It was Friday night, and I was late getting home from work . . . meeting ran over. When I walked in around 7:00, Harold was stretched out on the sofa with a twelve-pack of beer in the ice chest on the floor and five of the bottles already empty. Since I knew he had only beat me home by about an hour, I knew he had knocked back those five pretty quickly and was probably already useless in terms of helping me fix dinner and make out the shopping list for the supermarket. "You're drunk again," I said. "Screw you" was his response. We didn't talk again that night.

Argument #3

After a pretty nice evening together taking in a movie, I thought it would be a good time to reinforce Harold for sobriety. I said, "You are so much nicer when you're not drunk," thinking I was giving him a compliment. Well, he totally took it the wrong way and blew up at me, "There you go, riding me again, always complaining about drinking." I reacted and told him that if he wasn't such a drunk, I wouldn't need to complain, and from there the evening went straight down the tubes.

The next activity asks you to pick one of the three arguments you described in Activity 17 and map out a PIUS communication.

Activity 18. PIUS Planning

Select one argument from Activity 17 and rewrite your part so that it is Positive, leads in with "I" statements, shows Understanding of your drinker's struggles or point of view, and Shares responsibility with him/her.

Next time Harold and I have a nice evening when he doesn't drink, I am not even going to mention drinking. A more positive way to talk about the evening is to focus just on the fact that he is sober and not compare it to when he is not. Also, I think I need to let him know how happy being with him sober makes me feel and that I know it's not always easy for him. Finally, I should tell him that I do consider myself part of the situation and share the load with him. So, putting it together, I'll say something like, "Hon, thank you so much for this wonderful evening. I really love being with you like this [he knows I mean sober, don't need to say it], and I know it's not always easy for you so that makes it really special. What can I do to make things better for you?"

Having planned out her PIUS communication, DeeAnne rehearsed it mentally to make sure that when the time came, she was ready. Now you do the same.

Action Summary

The way you talk to your loved one not only reflects how you feel about him, but also sets the tone for his reactions to you. Practice using the PIUS communication style we discussed in this chapter. If need be, do some homework. Write down negative statements you have made to your loved one in the past and practice rewriting them in PIUS format. Then make sure you use this style to let your loved one know what you would like her to do and how you will respond to that behavior. The more clearly and "PIUS-ly" you communicate your requests and plans, the easier it will be for your loved one to cooperate.

Recap

- Phrase your communications in positive terms.
- Speak from the first person ("I").
- Make it clear that you understand your loved one's position.

• State your willingness to share responsibility for the situation about which you are talking.

———

Kathy and Jim: Developing a New Style

Kathy knew she had to find a way to tell Jim that she would no longer accept rough language directed at her or the kids. The problem was, anytime she had tried to tell him this in the past, he had responded with the very language she was trying to stop. This time she planned it differently. Instead of waiting for it to happen and calling it to his attention, she waited until they had an argument in which he did not swear. Then she said, "Jim, I know you are angry at me and agree we need to talk it out. But I first want to tell you how good I feel when we have these arguments without swearing at each other. Thank you so much." This took Jim by surprise. He almost forgot what he was angry about, and the rest of the argument lost much of its venom as he and Kathy calmly talked about the topic at hand.

chapter 10

Behavior Basics

Ladonna and Keith

Ladonna knew that Keith's drinking had gotten a lot worse over the past year—even if she did always defend him to her parents and insist that they were overreacting. In private she would beg him to cut back, plead with him to stop, and on a daily basis lately, get into a screaming match with him. Even though she knew she was right and he was wrong, she also knew that insisting on that point didn't help. They both needed to change, and she decided that because she was the sober one, she would go first.

This chapter is your "tool kit." Until now we have shown you how to target behaviors that need change and how to approach changing them. Here is where we pull together all the pieces to make it happen. You will recognize some of these strategies from examples in earlier chapters. Others will be things you already know and do. If a lot of this material is familiar, good. It will be easier to use. If the ideas are new to you, don't worry; you will learn them.

Rewards, Punishments, and the Big Chill

Psychologists and a lot of wise grandmothers know that the keys to behavior change are found in rewards, punishments, and the big chill. Psychologists call rewards "reinforcements," everyone calls punishment "punishment," and "the big chill" simply means ignoring unwanted behavior. (Psychologists call it "extinction.")

Rewards

The old saying "You catch more flies with honey than with vinegar" neatly sums up what rewards are all about. If you want someone to do something, give him a reward for doing it. Make that person feel good. The more often and powerfully someone is rewarded for behaving appropriately, the more likely she is to repeat that behavior.

For example, consider young Sammy whose mother is at the end of her rope trying to get him to keep his room tidy. After months of nagging and an ever-growing pile of junk on the floor, Mom decides bribery is in order. She tells Sammy that for each day he puts his dirty laundry in the hamper, makes his bed, and puts his toys in the toy box, he will receive a quarter. At the end of the week, Mom will take Sammy to the toy store where he can spend his earned money. Being a toy-loving kind of kid, Sammy thinks this is a terrific idea and becomes Mr. Clean.

Mom used a reward to bring Sammy around to her way of thinking. She may have called it bribery, but it was really a reward. Children have a natural need to play, and toys are a great way to satisfy that need. Thus, satisfying his desire for toys rewarded Sammy's behavior. The advantages of using rewards in a situation like this are clear. Mom stopped nagging Sammy so their relationship improved, Sammy willingly changed his behavior so Mom would lay off and give him a toy, and Mom had the satisfaction of being able, once again, to see the floor in Sammy's room.

There is one other thing to notice about the reward Mom chose for Sammy. She picked something that *Sammy* valued, not something she valued. *A reward is only a reward if the person for whom it is intended desires it.* Even if Mom had chosen her very most favorite vegetable, unless Sammy loved it too, it would not have worked as a reward.

You can apply the reward principle to your drinker and make it a pleasure for him to do what you want. Even if you could get your loved one to change by yelling at him, what would be more pleasant—yelling or making the change feel good? After all, your ultimate goal is to have your drinker change so the two of you can enjoy a happier relationship.

The more reinforcing a reward is, the more likely your loved one is to repeat the rewarded behavior. That is even how alcohol works. People know that if they drink, they will forget their troubles, be more romantic, feel less anxious, feel less depressed; in effect, alcohol will make them feel good. Unfortunately, that only hides the problems for now and creates more problems for later. But the initial expectation of immediate gratification prevents the individual from thinking about the longer-term consequences, so she just pays the piper later. That is how powerful positive rewards can be.

A good example of the use of reward was the way Kathy got Jim to come straight home from work at the end of chapter 2. Rather than pitching a fit about how awful it is when he stops for a drink with Charles, she held out a reward if he came straight home—his favorite meal, a smiling wife, and the company of his friend.

There is no limit to the variety of words, items, and situations that can be rewards. Anything that makes someone feel good/happy is a reward. That includes everything from a smile to a meal to sex to gifts to activities. If your drinker likes it, it's a reward. And remember, drinking is a reward too. The sum of *your* rewards must be greater than that of alcohol.

Rewarding people you love is easy to do. The tricky part is making sure you know what your loved one considers to be a reward. This can be particularly tough if the alcohol has changed him, and old pleasures have lost their attraction. Make a list of rewards you think your drinker will like. If you can come up with things your loved one might find more enjoyable than drinking, all the better. Minimally, make sure they are rewarding enough to get her attention. In the example below you can see that Ladonna wisely included her smiles, hugs, kisses, and pleasant words on her list. After all the fighting she and Keith had been doing, she rightly figured that simply showing him the side of her he first fell in love with would bring Keith pleasure. She was right! After reading Ladonna's list, write your own list in your notebook.

◆ Activity 19. Behavior Change to Reward

List the behaviors you want your loved one to do more often and the rewards that would be appropriate for each of them. It's a good idea to have more than one reward idea for each behavior in case the situation makes your original idea hard to carry out. It's also fine to reuse ideas.

Behavior	*Rewards*
Stay sober. No drinking.	• Tell Keith how much I enjoy his company when he's like this. Snuggle up to him on the sofa.
	• Tell him I love him and offer to make his favorite meal.
	• Slip into his favorite lingerie and invite him for an unexpected trip to the bedroom.

Stay home after dinner instead of going to the bar.	• Play Keith's favorite music and tell him how much I love spending the evening with him. Maybe ask him to dance in the living room like we used to when we were dating. • Offer to rub his back. • Surprise him with a shoot-'em-up movie and a big bowl of popcorn—his favorite "date" when we were younger.

Punishments

Everyone knows how to punish. Someone says or does something you dislike, so you say or do something that person dislikes to make him feel bad. When your loved one comes home higher than a kite, you yell or cry or throw something. That is punishment. Or is it?

If your relationship has deteriorated to the point where almost all of your interactions are negative, it just may be that your screaming or throwing are experienced by your drinker as rewards. Of course, this is not exactly the same as when you do something loving and she actively enjoys it. However, angry attention is often better than no attention at all. So when you pitch a fit, your drinker feels connected to you. Even if the connection is nasty and ugly, it is there nonetheless. Furthermore, if your interactions really escalate into highly emotional scenes, your drinker (and you, too) may experience a sort of adrenaline rush that may be rewarding. Also, the aftermath of a fight often involves making up and a sort of honeymoon period when everyone tries to be extra nice, and so the fight, in a sense, gets reinforced again. So the message here is to be very careful if you plan to use punishments to help your drinker to change. They can often backfire, and on top of that, they are not nearly as powerful at triggering lasting change as are rewards.

In most situations, you can get your point across equally or more effectively by using rewards or the big chill (see following section). Punishment should almost always be your last choice. If yelling and fighting has not been successful in the past, chances are slim to none it will be so now. More effective would be something we call "positive reframing." For instance, your loved one comes home drunk at two in the morning and wants to have sex with you. Instead of giving in just to shut him up or screaming and calling him a drunken pig, try this. Tell him you enjoy making love but only when he is sober and attentive to your needs, and you will be glad to have sex with him when he meets those conditions. In this way you have turned a potential punishment (rejection) into a promised reward when your loved one behaves appropriately.

The one type of punishment that we recommend you consider as you redesign your drinker's maps is withdrawal of reward. That means that rather than introducing something new and nasty into the situation, withdraw something positive. Kathy did this when she promised Jim a lovely dinner and pleasant evening if he came home by 5:30. When he failed to comply, she left him a cold meal and withdrew her company. He was punished but without the theatrics and potential danger of an argument.

We do have a word of caution about using punishment. Be alert to physical danger signals from your drinker. You know how far you can push her, so pay attention to your gut. There is no benefit in punishing your drinker to the point that a violent argument erupts or he slams out of the house in a rage. We know how tempting it can be to punish someone who has hurt you, but be careful that punishment does not backfire on you. Always keep your ultimate goal in mind and ask yourself whether this strategy will move you toward that goal or just give you the momentary satisfaction of revenge. If the latter, do not do it.

The Big Chill

Instead of using punishments when your loved one does something inappropriate, it is safer and more powerful to give her the big chill. It is very similar to withdrawal of a promised reward as we described in the previous section.

When your loved one misbehaves, let her know that you do not want to be around this behavior and then remove yourself. If there are other people in the situation with you, suggest you all go to another location or simply ignore the drinker. At all costs, do not allow her to drag you into an argument, which could ultimately be rewarding and move you away from, rather than toward, your goal.

For example, the two of you have snuggled together on the sofa for an evening of videos with the agreement that hot chocolate would be the drink of the night. About a third of the way into the movie your drinker pulls a beer out of the fridge. "Hon, remember we agreed no booze tonight so we could enjoy each other," you say. "I know," he answers, "but a beer would really taste good right now." "Please don't," you say. "Don't be such a nag," is his reply. At this point you could get into an argument with all the potential for nasty outcomes, not to mention that he still gets to spend the evening with you. Or you could say, "I'm sorry you are choosing to drink that beer instead of watching the rest of the movie with me. I'd rather be with you when you're not drinking, so I'm leaving now." With that, you get your coat, and leave for a friend's or relative's home or just leave the room. No fuss, no muss, and no rewards for drinking. You have given him the big chill and left him to thaw out on his own. That's a big message.

One More Thought

Before we end our discussion of rewards, punishments, and the big chill, we must add a word about the real world. Although our examples reflect real life, we have simplified them to make them clear teaching anecdotes. Your experiences with these strategies will sometimes be as smooth, or smoother, than what we describe and sometimes not. Figuring out new ways of living together is complicated, and once you apply them, they may take awhile to work. Sometimes plans backfire and you find yourself wondering if these methods are worth the effort. We can only tell you what experience has taught us.

If you have spent years trying to make a life with your drinker, you clearly value the relationship. That means the effort is indeed worthwhile. Very few of our clients have come into the program and experienced positive changes effortlessly. However, most have made some good changes happen. Sometimes it takes months of work but eventually the majority who use this approach are able to improve their quality of life, and many get their drinker to seek treatment. It just requires that you keep at it long enough to let the process work and keep working the process. Map out your strategies, track them, reevaluate them, and revise them. Then try again. You can make it happen.

Putting It Together

You've learned about rewards, punishments, the big chill, problem solving, mapping, goal setting, and PIUS communication. Now, how do you put it all together? Actually, it's easier than you might think. To begin with, look back at the drinking maps you made (in chapter 2) of your loved one's current behavior and the revisions you came up with. Then examine your responses for the following:

1. Is there anything you are doing that you thought would discourage drinking but isn't, or is actually rewarding it?
2. Is there a typical response of yours that rewards behavior that you do not want to reward? If so, how can you alter your behavior to use the big chill or, if appropriate and safe, punishment?
3. Are you punishing when you could be using the big chill or reward? Work on changing the situation into one where you focus on the positive and hold out a reward, rather than focus on the negative.
4. Are the revised ways you start discussions with or respond to your drinker phrased in positive "I" statements that show you understand how difficult change is for her and that share the responsibility for the situation?

As you answer each question, look for ways to improve your plans by using the techniques you have learned. Once you have plans that you feel pretty good about, practice them. Ideally, you would find someone to help you by acting out the situations described in the drinking maps. If you do not have anyone to role-play with, simply rehearse the plans in your imagination. You will be surprised at how effective mental rehearsal can be at improving your real life performance.

Now that you are ready to begin making some powerful changes in the way you interact with your drinker, it is important to let him know what is going on. No, you don't need to say that you have started a program to make him quit drinking. What you do need to say, though, is that you love him and want to improve your life together. Be sure to use positive communication to convey the message lovingly, with a focus on how you feel, and clearly show you understand the difficulties involved and share in the responsibility. Here are some examples.

- "I love you *("I" statement with your feeling)* so much that I get scared when I see you drinking. I know it's tough for you to quit *(understanding)*, so I'll stop nagging you about it, but I also can't bear to watch it anymore. I want things to get better so I won't be part of your drinking life anymore *(sharing responsibility)*. From now on, when you drink, I will leave the house until you are sober again."

- "I care for you and know how much stress you are under *(understanding/positive statement)*, but I can't handle what's going on *("I" statement)*. I need to make some changes in my life *("I" statement)*. I just can't go on the way we have been *(sharing responsibility)*. Are you willing to help me *(sharing responsibility)*?"

- "Our fights over drinking have upset this family long enough *(sharing responsibility)*. I know it bothers you as much as it does me *(understanding)*, and I'll do whatever it takes to help us *("I" statement/sharing responsibility)*. I love you and want to make a plan together to make our life happier *(positive/sharing responsibility)*."

- "The bills keep piling up and I'm worried *("I" statement)*. What can we do *(sharing responsibility)*? I love you so much and I'm afraid for our future *(positive/"I" statement)*."

IMPORTANT! If your drinker responds to one of these new communications positively by acknowledging the problem and the need for change, this may be a good time to suggest seeing a therapist together. We'll talk more about how to approach the idea of treatment in the next chapter but, for now, keep in mind that any remorse on her part offers an excellent opportunity for you to broach the subject. If you do and she reacts negatively, drop it for now. There will be other opportunities—and more successful attempts.

Try It, You'll Like It

When all is said and done, you are asking yourself and your drinker to change the way the two of you live by changing day-to-day behavior. It can be scary—particularly for the person who is alcohol dependent and facing a future without his emotional crutch. Rather than trying to convince anyone to change something "forever," ask for small, comfortable changes. Ask your drinker to consider not drinking this *one* visit from your parents or to commit only to coming home in time for dinner on Monday this week. Make it small to make it achievable. It will be easier to get a commitment that way, and the chances of that commitment being honored will be greater. Your task will be to ensure that following through on her promise is equal to or more rewarding than drinking.

There are a thousand and one areas in which you can take the "try it, you'll like it" approach. Anytime you ask for a change from your drinker, think about how you can make that change a baby step he can easily take and you can reward. Below are examples of how our clients have successfully used this approach over the years.

- Instead of trying to get someone to commit to helping keep the entire house tidy forever, focus on one behavior at a time: "Honey, I know it upsets you when I leave my makeup in the bathroom sink, so I cleared it off. If you will keep your wet towels on the rack and off the floor, I'll promise to keep my makeup off the sink." When you have the towel challenge whipped, you can tackle the dinner dishes and so on.

- Changing the way a parent relates to a small child is no easier than changing the way you and your drinker relate to one another. If you want to improve your drinker's behavior toward your children, avoid asking her to "be nicer" or "more understanding." Those are great big global changes and hard to define. Rather, ask for one small behavior change. For example, you might say, "It upsets me terribly when you yell at Billy about his room. If you try to calmly tell him when it's too messy, I'll help him keep it tidy."

- More couples argue about money than just about anything else. This can be a particularly bad problem if one member of the couple is a problem drinker who is either unemployed or spends money inappropriately. Again, it is easier to ask for one little behavior modification than to change the drinker's entire style. A good first step would sound like this: "I understand that you are under a lot of pressure, and I don't want to add to it. I am worried about being able to pay the bills though. Do you think we could plan out a household budget so we have enough to run the house?"

- "You just don't talk to me anymore" has never, to our knowledge, resulted in an increase in communication. If you want to open the lines of communication, ask for one small change such as, "Lately we just haven't been on the same page. I'd like to spend some time with you just talking about our relationship. Can we set aside just thirty minutes tomorrow morning to talk?" There is no need to ask for a monthlong commitment to this activity. In fact, there is no need to insist on thirty minutes. Ten will do as well. Ask for an amount of time and a number of days that you think will be easy for your drinker. Then, no matter how the conversations go, reward the fact that your loved one took the time to do this for you. A kiss, hug, or simply a heartfelt thank-you opens him up to further communications.

• Sex and affectionate displays are often the first to fall by the wayside of problem drinking. If your drinker has bemoaned your lack of willingness and you have no interest in kissing a bottle, work on one sober kiss at a time. Make coming to bed sober as attractive as you can. For instance, "If you come home right after work, I'll have my mother watch the kids and I'll wear that new teddy you like so much. One thing may lead to another. . . . What do you say?"

Notice how in all of the examples the speaker uses the PIUS pattern. The communications are positive and clearly share responsibility for the situation. When relevant, they demonstrate understanding and employ "I" statements. It is also important to be aware that each of these speakers first made sure the rewards they offered were appealing to their drinkers. Remember, young Sammy would not have cleaned his room for the promise of eggplant—even if it *is* his mother's favorite food.

Track Yourself

When clients work with us at the clinic, they have the luxury of coming into the office regularly and reviewing their progress—what they tried, what went right, what went wrong, and how they can improve it. Unfortunately, we do not have the luxury of meeting with you privately and coaching you through this process. However, we can tell you about the next best thing. Keep a written record of your plans, how/when you use them, what happens, and how you revise them. In other words, keep track of yourself just as you would if we were meeting regularly to review your outcomes.

Because you are so intimately involved in everything that happens, it will be particularly difficult for you to objectively analyze what happens by just reviewing it mentally. Putting it down on paper is the best way to help you take a step back and get a clear picture of how your behavior affects your drinker. Keep a record of everything that happens. You will find that as time goes on it becomes easier to remember to write things down and that you will come to enjoy reviewing your notes. After all, they are the maps you are following to a happier future.

It is also a good idea to periodically repeat the baseline activities from chapter 2. Doing so will give you a yardstick against which to measure the changes in your drinker and in your life. Chances are the results will be satisfying. If not, chapter 12 talks about what options you have to improve your life even if your drinker does not change.

Action Summary

You now have additional tools that will help you to make powerful and satisfying changes in your life. For each drinking sequence you map, plan your strategies for changing the course of events. Make rewards your most well-used tool and look for opportunities to reward your drinker for positive behaviors. Remember, too, that positive behaviors can also simply be the absence of negative behaviors. *Every instance in which your loved one is sober is reason for reward.* Use your smiles, your words, and your actions to make sobriety more attractive than drinking.

Recap

- Rewards must be attractive to their target.
- Punishment is not nearly as effective for achieving long-lasting behavior change as is reward.
- The big chill (extinction) is a helpful complement to reward.
- Use all the tools you have learned to make *not* drinking equal to or more attractive than drinking to your loved one.

Kathy and Jim: Making Changes

Kathy finally began to feel like she was in charge of her life after she mapped out Jim's three most common drinking sequences, from triggers to consequences, and planned exactly how she would handle each one. Much as she was tempted to dwell on making Jim see what a jerk he was, Kathy forced herself to focus on the things she wanted him to do, rather than not do, and found positive ways to explain them to him.

One frequent argument Jim and Kathy would have was over how they were raising their son, Ted. Jim felt Kathy was too soft on him and would constantly yell at them both about Ted's behavior. Kathy felt that with all the stress their kids had to live under because of Jim's drinking, they should cut the kids a little slack on things like keeping their rooms neat and phone use.

Ted, their eldest at eleven years old, seemed to go out of his way to misbehave in order to get Jim's attention. Kathy knew that if Jim only showed Ted a little affection, his behavior would improve. However, in spite of all the lecturing and arguing, Jim would still blow up whenever Ted took the smallest step out of line. In fact, Kathy had mapped out a typical sequence: Jim comes in the door from work, and Ted runs up to tell his dad about some event of the day. Jim tells Ted to give him a chance to get his coat off and pour a drink, and Ted withdraws to mope on the sidelines. Within moments Ted manages to knock something over (sometimes his little sister) or scatter schoolwork or toys across the kitchen table. Jim's reaction is almost inevitably to yell at the boy, demanding to know "What the hell is wrong with you?" Ted cries and slams the door of his room shut. Jim pounds on the door and tells Ted not to come out until he tells him to. Any hope of spending a good time together that evening is shot.

Once Kathy clearly saw the relationship between Jim's and Ted's behavior, she planned better ways to organize their end-of-the-day routine. For starters, she talked to Ted about waiting until Daddy had been home and was settled on the sofa with his shoes off before approaching him with stories of the sixth grade. Then she focused on injecting a little positive interaction into Jim and Ted's relationship. Rather than trying to convince Jim that he needed to be more positive with his son if he wanted the kid to improve his own behavior, she approached it by appealing to his sense of fatherhood (and his ego) and putting a positive slant on the situation. She said, "Jim, I know how much Ted means to you, and he loves spending time with you too. He really looks up to you. Why don't you come straight home from work tonight and the two of you can go to the Pizza Factory for supper. You guys can play some video games and get away from the chaos around here. I'll stay home with the little ones, and you and Ted go enjoy each other."

Jim's response to Kathy's invitation to have fun with his son was surprising to Kathy. She had expected him to reject the idea because he was tired after work, needed to stop at the tavern to discuss something with the guys, knew Ted would misbehave at the restaurant, or any number of other excuses he had used in the past to avoid time with the kids. This time, however, he said *yes*. Kathy almost started arguing with him about it out of sheer habit. But she didn't. Instead, she hugged him and told him that Ted would be thrilled. She also telephoned him at work about twenty minutes before quitting time to remind him of his plans for that evening and to tell him Ted was so excited that he had already completed all his homework and straightened up his room. Jim laughed and said he'd be home right after work—and he was.

chapter 11

Treatment

Linda and Ron

Linda has been worried about Ron, her twin brother, since they were juniors in high school. Now, sharing an apartment at college, she was panicked as she watched him party all night, sleep through his morning classes, and generally let his life go down the drain. Whenever she tried to talk to him about it, he firmly reminded her that she was his sister and not his mother. Inevitably, when she'd suggest he talk to one of the mental health counselors on campus, he'd explode and storm out of the apartment. By changing the way she talked to him and by learning to stop enabling his drinking, she was able to cut their fights way down and restore some harmony in their relationship. However, she was still convinced that Ron's drinking was not just "college fun," as he put it, and that it required professional help.

In many respects, getting your drinker into treatment is both the high point and the low point of this journey. It represents the high point because, for many drinkers, treatment is the only way they can successfully learn to live without liquor. It can also be the low point because, as you know, change is tough, and your loved one will struggle in treatment. Of course, your drinker's struggles also become your struggles and so, as always, your effort continues to be critical to the mix.

Getting your drinker into treatment requires the same attention to detail and planning as everything else you have done so far. Most people who abuse alcohol are, at best, ambivalent about entering treatment. Even at the point where they become aware of how much pain and suffering their drinking causes, the thought of quitting is scary. You will need to be sensitive to these fears as you proceed.

Reasons to Drink

There are both costs and benefits for your drinker to continue drinking. The costs are clear and you can list them better than we can. However, the benefits may be less obvious but are equally important. Each individual has a unique experience with alcohol, but it is helpful to review some of the more common reasons drinkers have for not quitting. Some, all, or none of these may be true for your loved one. An important task for you is to figure out what benefits your drinker enjoys. If possible, talk to him about this. If not, use the intimate knowledge you have, your powers of observation, and your critical thinking abilities. Activity 20 will help with this. Read how Linda completed the activity for Ron's drinking and then use your notebook to complete your own activity.

◆ Activity 20. Why Drink?

The following list will help get your creative insight flowing. Check off the drinking reasons that you think may apply to your drinker. Add to the list as you reflect on your drinker's behavior or talk to him/her about it. After reviewing your list, write a summary.

_X_ Alcohol tastes good.

_X_ Alcohol feels good.

_____ Getting high allows him/her to avoid unpleasant feelings.

_____ Getting high allows him/her to avoid unpleasant situations.

_X_ Drinking gives him/her confidence in social situations.

_____ Drinking gives him/her confidence in romantic situations.

_____ Drinking relieves stress.

_X_ Drinking is a shared pastime with friends and/or family.

_____ Drinking is the only hobby he/she has.

_____ Drinking is a good excuse for not being able to work.

_____ Drinking is the easiest way to escape pain or boredom.

_____ Drinking numbs bad feelings.

_____ Others?

When he's not drinking, Ron is basically a shy guy. So in addition to liking the taste of alcohol, he enjoys the "courage in a bottle" it gives him socially. All this has made it really easy for him to get into a drinking habit. Now, I'm figuring he also has a physical addiction to the alcohol, so there's both emotional and physical attractions that keep him drinking.

Remember, if you ask your loved one to give up drinking, you must be ready to help her find something equally rewarding with which to replace it.

In Chapter 2 you estimated how much time your loved one spends on drinking and drinking-related activities. If he gives up those activities, he will need to fill his time with some healthier activities. Be prepared to offer your drinker other, equally rewarding activities to select from. For instance, if she spends an hour or two each day after work socializing with friends at the bar, your drinker will need some other, non-drinking social activity to fill that time. The same goes for weekend and evening hours. Leaving a void will only leave a hole crying to be filled—and if left to his own devices, your drinker will fill it with the old, familiar drink. Your job at this stage of the game is to give your loved one as many attractive reasons not to drink as he can find to drink.

Get ready for your loved one's sobriety and help it along by preparing a list of nondrinking, rewarding activities that can be enjoyed in place of drinking. Make sure the activities you select are appealing to your loved one and not only to yourself. Even if you do not see the attraction in liquor, remember that it fulfills many needs for your drinker. Plan accordingly. In fact, consult the expert on this. Talk to your loved one about it. Use your PIUS communication style to ask what you can do together that would be pleasurable enough to forgo liquor for that period. Activity 21 will help you make this list. Review Linda's list below in the example, then write down your own list in your notebook.

Activity 21. Activities Worth Staying Sober For

- *Early morning jogs (Ron loved track in high school)*
- *All-night heart-to-heart chats with me (we used to do this regularly before I became so angry about his drinking)*
- *Skateboarding around campus after the crowds thin in the evening*
- *Loading up with popcorn to watch foreign films at the local cinema*

The nondrinking activities you prepare for your loved one's sobriety are also powerful incentives toward that sobriety. As you work on drinking maps and make plans to encourage sobriety, use these activities as incentives and rewards. You do not need to wait until your loved one is in treatment to begin enjoying these nondrinking times together. Offer her the pleasure of your company in exchange for sobriety for however long and however often your loved one can remain sober. With enough of these positive interactions, extended sobriety and, ultimately, treatment will follow.

Selecting Treatment

If you do nothing else, do this: *Have treatment ready to go the instant your loved one says he is interested.* That interest will peak and then dissolve if you do not seize the moment. For every reason you can think of to seek sobriety, your loved one has two to avoid it. When the scales finally tip in favor of her thinking about treatment, you cannot afford to let that balance shift again while you search for a suitable program.

A number of treatment options are available. While all have their fans, not all have been demonstrated to produce consistent results. We will describe the most popular treatment options and tell you what is known about their effectiveness. Keep in mind, however, that once your loved one is willing to enter treatment, you may have to alter your choice to accommodate his preferences. Think about what you know about your drinker's tastes and style as you make your selection.

The first step in exploring treatment options is to understand the difference between treatment and support. When we talk about "treatment," we are referring to an active intervention program that takes your loved one by the hand and *teaches* her how to beat liquor. This is different from support groups that provide encouragement and crisis intervention but do not teach and help the individual practice new nondrinking behaviors. We are talking about specific skills here; a treatment program must teach the person skills to resist drinking and to rebuild his life. Preferably, the program will also actively involve the drinker's loved ones just as we have reached out to your drinker by helping you through this book. Thus, as you evaluate treatment programs, ask specifically how they intend to teach your loved one to live without or manage alcohol. If you do not hear specific strategies that clearly target problem behaviors, keep looking.

Get Your Loved One Sober: Alternatives to Nagging, Pleading, and Threatening is based on a model that research has proven to be effective. The generic description of the program you have been working through is cognitive-behavioral therapy or skills-training therapy. At our clinic, the program is called Community Reinforcement and Family Training (CRAFT) and grew out of an earlier program called Community Reinforcement Approach (CRA), which directly treats the drinker. CRA continues to be the treatment of choice in our clinic and has helped a great number of problem drinkers replace alcohol with a positive lifestyle.*

You can find programs similar to CRA and complementary to what you have been doing here by looking for treatments that include phrases in their descriptions such as "social skills training," "behavioral marital therapy," "cognitive-behavioral treatment," "rational-emotive therapy," "motivational treatment," or "solution-focused therapy." It is important to keep in mind that different treatment centers and providers will have their own "spin," so to speak, on the treatment models. That is, they will offer programs of different lengths, different delivery formats (individual, family, group), and likely use slightly different language to describe what may well amount to the same treatments. As you investigate the various options in your community, remember that you are looking for treatment to help your loved one figure out the triggers and reinforcers of her unhealthy behaviors, teach her how to change the triggers and reinforcers that can be changed, and teach her how to change her responses to those that cannot.

There are hundreds of treatment programs from which to choose, and it is beyond the scope of this book to even begin

---

*For a detailed description of CRA, please see: Meyers, R. J., and J. E. Smith. 1995. *Clinical guide to alcohol treatment: The community reinforcement approach.* New York: Guilford Press.

to describe each and every one. Suffice it to say, however, that the program you select should minimally address the three skills just listed and also be a comfortable place for you and your loved one. Do not be shy to call around, ask questions, interview providers, and ask about ancillary services the program may offer. You are the "customer" and have the right to make sure that you are selecting the best "product" for you and your loved one. Use the phone directory and look up alcohol and drug rehabilitation or mental health centers. Also check with the local state alcohol and drug agency.

Over the years there has been much debate about whether inpatient or outpatient treatment works best. From a cost-effectiveness standpoint, however, it does not look as though inpatient therapy (which is considerably more expensive than outpatient) adds much to success rates (Miller and Hester 1986). Nonetheless, you should explore all options, as there is no single best way, and what works or does not work for your neighbor may or may not work for you. Before you set your heart on any one facility, however, check with your health insurance to see whether it is covered.

There is a fair degree of variability in outpatient programs. In addition to the different approaches they may take, you also have choices about the structure. They might offer once a week sessions for individuals, group therapy, or evening sessions to accommodate work schedules. Many programs also provide day treatment programs that require attendance from morning to mid- to late-afternoon each day. Many outpatient programs require patients to attend self-help groups such as Alcoholics Anonymous (AA) in addition to therapy, and some outpatient groups use a Twelve Step format as their treatment. The bottom line on all treatments is that they cannot work if the drinker does not *attend and participate* long enough to let them work.

In addition to an active treatment program, many people

find it helpful to make use of a good support group such as Alcoholics Anonymous (AA) and Narcotics Anonymous (NA) for your loved one, and Al-Anon and Nar-Anon for you. In fact, the social support and help with structuring time that formerly was spent drinking or drugging is tremendously helpful to many people.

Interview Treatment Providers

Once you decide on the best approach for you and your drinker, take the time to interview a few different treatment providers who fit your ideal model. Different therapists using the same approach will work differently with different clients. Let the therapists you want to interview know what you are doing. Most will be willing to meet with you (often without charge) to discuss their approach. At minimum, the provider should be willing to spend a few minutes with you on the telephone answering your questions about his approach.

When you interview treatment providers, ask any questions that come to mind, and voice your concerns. (In fact, prepare a list of questions ahead of time so that you don't overlook anything.) A good facility (or therapist) will not only welcome your questions but will help you think of questions if you are unsure about what to ask. It is in the facility's best interest to ensure that all clients understand what it has to offer and how the program works.

The more obvious questions to ask include the following:

- How much does the program cost?
- Does my insurance cover it?
- How long is each session?
- How frequently will my loved one attend sessions?

You will also want to know whether treatment is given in groups only or whether there are options for individual, couple, and family therapy.

If your loved one has been a heavy drinker for a long time and shows signs of physical dependence, she might need to be admitted to a hospital or detoxification unit before treatment can begin. You should find out if the treatment facility has access to this type of medical support. If not, ask how you could arrange for it in addition to psychotherapy.

Drinking often masks other problems such as depression or anxiety disorders, and when an individual stops drinking, these problems become evident. Thus, it is important to ensure that the program has the appropriate personnel to deal with mental health issues. In some cases, the individual will require medications to help him through the difficult withdrawal and readjustment period.

Ask the therapist to describe her philosophy and give you a detailed description about the treatment itself. Our recommendation, based on scientific research, is that you seek treatments that fall into the categories of behavioral therapy or cognitive-behavioral therapy, either for the individual or couple or family. If you are considering another approach, or someone is trying to talk you into one, ask this person to give you a list of the published outcome research supporting the treatment. Find out as much as you can before deciding.

You will also want to know what the therapist's qualifications are. Is the therapist a certified alcohol counselor or a licensed psychotherapist? If not, we would recommend looking elsewhere. You should also find out how long the individual has been working with problem drinkers. There is no perfect amount of experience to look for, but unwillingness to give you this information is a flag to look elsewhere. There are pros and cons to more- and less-experienced therapists. More experience can translate into greater effectiveness, but newly graduated therapists tend to be more up-to-date in the field. It all comes down to finding someone you are comfortable with and feel confident in.

Finally, ask how the therapist plans to involve you in the

program. If she seems surprised at the question, this is not the therapist for you. You need someone who will work with both of you (and other family members as needed) to change not only the drinker but also the drinker's environment. Changing one without the other is not a recipe for success.

Windows of Opportunity

With treatment ready for when your loved one indicates readiness, you can begin to start looking for those windows of opportunity. That's right. You do not rush home to inform your drinker that you have found a fabulous treatment plan. If you have ever tried this before, you know what the response is likely to be.

The best way to avoid rejection and increase the likelihood your drinker will be open to the idea of treatment is to watch for those moments when his motivation peaks. Those might be times your loved one is particularly disgusted with himself or when the two of you are getting along particularly well and your drinker wants to please you. You know your drinker best so be alert for receptive moments.

Just as you carefully plan and practice the changes you make to improve the way you relate to your drinker, finding the windows of opportunity to suggest treatment also requires careful thought. As we said, you know your drinker best, so we cannot tell you what to look for. However, we can guide your thinking with the questions in Activity 22. Linda was pleasantly surprised to realize that there were actually a number of conditions under which she thought Ron would be receptive to the idea of therapy. Read her answers in the example and then write down your answers in your notebook.

Activity 22. Open That Window

1. When would your drinker be most likely to try something new in the way of treatment? *Probably toward the end of one of our late-night relaxed chats.*

2. Is there a particular time of day he/she is most relaxed? *Late night.*

3. Would your loved one be most open to discussing the possibility of treatment when the two of you are alone or with others? If with others, with whom? *Alone.*

4. Would your drinker be most open to treatment after a few days of sobriety or while suffering the aftermath of a major drunk? *I think when he's got a hangover.*

5. Is your drinker most open to your suggestions when the two of you have not fought for a few days or when making up from a fight? *When we've not fought for a few days.*

6. Would your loved one be willing to enter treatment if it were for your relationship? (This would be what we call a "backdoor" approach—doing it to improve the relationship and coincidentally also improving the drinker's health and behavior.) *Don't think this is relevant.*

7. Review past attempts to get your loved one into treatment. What worked? What did not? *Tried plenty of times to talk him into it, argued, yelled, belittled. Nothing worked.*

Once you identify a few situations (or moods) that you think would be conducive to suggesting treatment, play various scenarios through your mind. Try to anticipate with as much detail as possible what the setting will be, what you will say, and how your drinker might respond. Be sure to think it through. What will you say if she responds positively, and what will you say if she responds negatively? In other words, plan, plan, plan!

For example, you may have noticed that your drinker feels really guilty after being ugly toward you, and you think this would be a good time to suggest treatment. The conversation might go something like this.

Drinker: I didn't know what I was doing. I'm so sorry. How can I make it up to you?

You: Actually, there is something you can do. I know you didn't mean to hurt me, but you did. I have a therapist who can help us stop doing this. I really want us to go together. Would you be willing to give it a try?

Drinker: Yeah, I guess so.

You: Thank you so much. I'll call right now for an appointment.

If the drinker hesitates, a good response would be the following:

You: Let's go just once or twice to see if it helps. If you really don't like it, we can stop.

Drinker: Okay, but I'm not promising anything.

You: That's okay. I just really appreciate your willingness to consider it. That makes me feel good.

The fact is that the drinker will stop treatment anyhow if he dislikes it, so there is no point in insisting. Your loved one has control over where and when he does what—so acknowledge that control. Demanding that someone does something typically results in his wanting to do just the opposite. In our experience, we have found that once the drinker gets into treatment and the therapist eases his fears, the person accepts help. It is getting him in the door the first time that is hard.

It is best not to *ask* if your loved one wants to go for help. Make the statement matter-of-fact—but do so in a nurturing, responsibility-sharing way rather than a dictatorial one. Offer treatment as something that will make your life together better rather than as something that will fix your loved one's "defect." Here is another example.

It is Saturday morning and you are home with your loved one. Although she drank last night, she isn't hungover and is in a good mood. You offer to fix her favorite breakfast and keep the mood upbeat as you talk about common interests. If your loved one's good mood continues and you feel the time is right, you may have this conversation:

You:	It sure is peaceful around here this morning. I enjoy the quiet.
Drinker:	Yes, it is peaceful this morning.
You:	I have been doing some thinking lately. I feel that things have been going better between us, but I would like them to get even better. I really love you.
Drinker:	I love you too.
You:	I have been going to a therapist to help me sort things out. I think it's helping.
Drinker:	I didn't know you were going to a therapist. What's going on?
You:	Well, I love you so much I want to do everything I can to make our life happier. Wouldn't you like to make our life together happier?
Drinker:	I hope this isn't going where I think it's going. Things are going fine this morning. Can't you just leave things alone?
You:	I just want things to be as good as they can be. Would you be willing to come with me

	just once to meet my therapist? Do it for us.
Drinker:	Is this some sort of marriage counseling? We don't need that crap; we're doing fine.
You:	We are doing fine, but we can do better. Going with me once isn't going to hurt you.
Drinker:	I'll think about it. Can we change the subject now?
You:	Sure. We can talk about it later.

In this example we model how to keep the interaction positive and avoid confrontation. Remember, go with the flow. Don't force the issue if your loved one resists. Once the ice is broken, it will be easier to raise the subject the next time a window of opportunity opens. It may take several tries until your loved one accepts help, but if you avoid fighting over the subject, you can continue to raise the issue until your loved one agrees.

You can even continue to up the ante according to your sense of the situation. You can become more forceful (not confrontational) as you sense his resistance weakening, or you can increase the promised rewards. You can also decrease what you are asking of your drinker by moving from "come to therapy with me" to "come for one session" or simply "talk to my therapist on the telephone and find out what she has to offer." Some drinkers are also enticed to meet the therapist by being told that the therapist has heard so much about them, the therapist just wants to meet them. There is no limit on how creative you can become to prop that window of opportunity open and entice your drinker to step through.

In working with clients over the years, we have found a few strategies that work well with most people. As always, though, evaluate each one for how appropriate it is to your situation. Only the first two suggestions apply to everyone.

1. Safety first. No matter how carefully you plan your treatment suggestions, abandon your plans in a flash if your drinker shows signs of turning violent. Drop the subject, soothe him, and save your breath for next time. There *will* be a next time and the goal is for you to be able to take advantage of it.

2. Make sure the therapist and program you have selected will feel comfortable to your drinker. That is, don't arrange an evangelical therapist for an atheist drinker or group sessions for someone who suffers social anxiety. Try to find a comfortable match between the therapy/therapist and your loved one. On the other hand, be prepared and prepare your drinker for a tough process. Change, as you know, is tough. However, keep in mind that the objective here is happiness, and most things worth having do have a cost.

3. If you are in therapy, it sometimes helps to let your drinker know and invite her to join you. Remember, though, to use a PIUS communication and make it a positive invitation. You might say something like, "I've been in therapy because I'm having a hard time, and it would be great if you could come too to help me. . . . My therapist would love to meet you."

4. Another option if you are in therapy is to have your therapist call your loved one with an invitation to attend a session. Again, the invitation should be positive in that the therapist's objective is to meet an important person in your life to better understand *your* relationship. Furthermore, ask your

therapist to simply invite your drinker to *one* session. If the session goes smoothly and your drinker seems comfortable, then he would be asked to return for a second session.

5. If you are not in therapy, you can introduce the topic by asking your drinker if she would be willing to talk to a therapist with you. Instead of laying everything on the drinker's shoulders ("You need treatment because you are a drunk"), emphasize your commitment to the relationship and to doing what it takes to live happily together ("I really want to be a better partner in this marriage, and it would help me if you came to talk to a therapist with me.") Once your loved one has agreed to work on improving your life together, addressing alcohol will become a natural part of that process.

6. If the drinker has refused to come to treatment but knows you are involved in a program, you may give him a card with a scheduled appointment for him. This sometimes carries more weight than a verbal invitation. If your loved one misses the appointment, you can always discuss it later and possibly make another.

7. You may mention that you heard about a new/effective/interesting program and invite your loved one to try it with you—no strings attached.

8. If your loved one has been sick, you can say you are concerned about her health and would she at least seek help for the physical problems.

9. Appeal to your loved one's loves. Ask him to get help for job security, the children, your marriage, your sex life, his health, and so on. Often, the most powerful incentive for change is fear of losing one's greatest loves.

10. If your drinker is consistently resistant to the idea of treatment, you might try just discussing treatment with her. That is, instead of recommending it, ask your loved one under what conditions she would think treatment is appropriate. This conversation may go nowhere, but it may also give the two of you an opportunity to calmly discuss your current situation and compare how similarly or differently you perceive it. More important, you learn what button presses will motivate your drinker. For instance, she might say that as long as your marriage is holding together as well as it is, there is no need to make any changes. Or your loved one may think that her drinking really isn't causing anyone great pain. In both situations, you have the opportunity to PIUS-ly give your loved one the straight scoop.

Clients often worry that if they set up everything as we have instructed, finding out that they had prearranged treatment might make their drinkers feel manipulated. This is certainly possible. However, remember that we are encouraging you to be honest with your drinker from the start. You have stopped pretending that life as it has been is acceptable to you. You have told him when you are unwilling to fix his messes and under what circumstances you enjoy being with him. At some point in the process, it is also likely that you have let your loved one know that you are in therapy and are hoping that the personal growth you experience will also help your relationship grow. Tell her that you are in treatment and you have a therapist that is helping work out some problems. You can then ask her to go with you to therapy, and at that point you can have it prearranged that you leave the session and it becomes her treatment, or during therapy it could be suggested that she get her "own" therapist. There are many alternatives of this scenario. If you offer help in the context of loving steps you have taken to make sure your loved one has choices should he want to exercise them, he is not likely to feel manipulated. If he does react angrily, back off and tell him that you did not mean to pressure him—that you were only trying to have options available should he want them.

When the Window Slams Shut

For all your careful planning and patient waiting for that window of opportunity to open, there remains the possibility that your drinker will slam it shut. Everything will be perfect, the two of you will be on a really positive roll, you will lovingly and clearly raise the topic, and your drinker will explode. Or you get your drinker all the way to the waiting room of your therapist's office, and she gets cold feet and stomps out. What do you do? Simple. You do the same things you did to get her there in the first place. You thank her for considering it, remind her how much you love her and enjoy being with her when she is sober, and you plan and wait for another window of opportunity. It happens.

The beautiful thing about windows (of opportunity as well as those that let in fresh air) is that they can open, shut, open, shut, and open again. If you need to back off, that's okay. The fact that the window opened, however briefly, means it *can* open. Just review your strategy to see if you can improve it and bide your time. Most of the people who use this program get their drinker to at least try treatment. Remember, this is much like a road trip. Change takes time and the path meanders along its way. Getting your drinker into treatment often takes repeated attempts, but it can be done.

Supporting Treatment

When your loved one enters treatment, it is important that you continue to practice the new interaction style you have been working on. In fact, your help will be needed more than ever. You know from your experience how difficult it can be to change long-standing habits and how easy it is to become discouraged and give in to the old familiar patterns. Now imagine how difficult change can be with the added challenge of trying to give up a drug (or drugs) that affect not only the mind but the body as well. In a word—hellacious.

More than a few drinkers have abandoned treatment because it was too difficult to change themselves while their environment remained the same. You have made some excellent changes in your drinker's environment at this point. It is critical that you continue to use rewards, to communicate using the PIUS style, and to pay attention to the triggers and patterns that lead to drinking, arguments, and other difficult situations. Your job from this point on will be to continue working on improving the way the two of you interact and to support treatment. You cannot simply send your drinker off to be "fixed." You must be an active supporter and, if necessary, an involved participant in treatment.

Depending on the type of program your loved one enters, your role will vary. Our hope is that he becomes involved with an active treatment program that focuses not only on eliminating the drinking problem, but also on replacing drinking with other healthier, more productive behavior patterns. If you are not in couples therapy, get your loved one's okay to talk to his therapist. Ask how you can help. Better yet, ask your loved one how you can help. You may be amazed at the types of help an individual asks for that might never have occurred to you.

Two of the universally appropriate ways to support treatment are to remove obstacles to treatment and to reward your loved one for going. Make it easy to go by ensuring child-care duties are covered, transportation is available, other events are not scheduled for that time, and whatever else you can think of to remove obstacles. Reward your loved one by telling her that you are proud, pleased, impressed, delighted, or otherwise thrilled with her for making the effort. Do not dwell on how bad things used to be. Rather, focus on the positive change and your bright future. Make being in treatment as easy as you can.

When to Involve a Medical Professional

In most cases, your best bet for treatment is a licensed mental health worker (clinical psychologist, clinical social worker, certified alcohol counselor). These people are trained to help the problem drinker find healthier ways of coping with life. However, there are instances in which the assistance of a medical professional such as a physician or psychiatrist is recommended.

If your loved one is drinking large quantities of liquor (more than five or six drinks per day for many weeks), he may need medical detoxification (detox) to help with withdrawal symptoms. Past experience is your best guide; if your loved one had withdrawal symptoms when giving up alcohol or drugs in the past, it is likely that she will need medical detox this time. Typically, medical detox takes three to five days and can be done either on an inpatient or outpatient basis, depending on the severity and on the resources available in your community. During detox, medical personnel will monitor your loved one and provide medications to help him get through the delusions, tremors, seizures, and other withdrawal symptoms that may begin a number of hours after the last drink. Beware, though, that psychological withdrawal will take considerably longer than physical. Psychotherapy is essential to deal with the emotional stress of giving up liquor and adjusting to a new lifestyle. Getting past the physical withdrawal is only the first step.

Other instances in which a medical professional should be involved include the presence of liver problems (clues to this include a distended stomach, yellow tint to the skin and eyes, and wounds that refuse to heal), multiple drug use, or a history of emotional or psychiatric problems requiring medication. This list is by no means definitive. If you have any doubt as to the health status of your loved one or her ability to handle the stresses of giving up alcohol, consult a physician.

Help for the Rest of the Family

Most likely, other family members have also been adversely affected by alcohol, and it's important to seek family therapy or individual help for those family members. Al-Anon is a good resource for family members who need the support and empathy of others who have lived, or are living, through similar situations. Most communities have several Al-Anon chapters listed in the phone book.

Roll with the Punches

As thrilled as you are when your loved one enters treatment, keep in mind how difficult the process may be for him. Once the initial self-satisfaction of having taken this step wears off (possibly within hours or days), your loved one will be hit with the reality of giving up an old, dearly loved friend. It will be tough, and there are surely going to be times that your loved one takes it out on you. After all, it was *your* dissatisfaction with the drinker's life that started the whole change process.

Accept that responsibility (secretly pat yourself on the back) and keep your goal in mind. You can put up with his temporary resentment to eventually live the life you deserve. As long as you keep yourself safe—it is too early to toss your safety plan yet—and continue to use all the strategies you have been practicing, you can get through this. So can your loved one.

Another warning we must give you is that more drinkers drop out of treatment than stay in—at least initially. It is very common for people to go in and out of treatment a number of times before they really begin to make lasting changes. Do not lose heart if your loved one enters treatment only to drop out after a short time. All the changes you have made figure into the success equation and even a treatment drop-out cannot negate them. Keep on working to make your life more pleasant and to reward your loved one for nondrinking behaviors. Continue to take care of yourself and to avoid making it easy for your loved one to drink without consequences. It may take a number of tries, but eventually there is a very good likelihood that your loved one will come around. In the meantime, keep your eye on the positive changes you have accomplished and enjoy them.

At some point you may decide that you have done all you can and tried as many times as you care to. You will have to decide whether to pull the plug on the relationship if your drinker does not change. At that point, you may want to use this decision as one last attempt to motivate your drinker into treatment by telling her that you are leaving unless changes are made. However, if you do so, make sure you are ready to follow through on your threat. Otherwise, you lose future credibility. Idle threats just give the drinker more power.

Action Summary

As we said earlier, the most critical piece of what you accomplish in this step is to have treatment ready to go as soon as your loved one indicates he is open to the idea. You must be able to get the drinker to a therapist within twenty-four to forty-eight hours of his agreeing to the idea. In our experience, this is about the maximum length of time the window will remain open. In fact, minutes after your loved one says, "I do need treatment," motivation may begin to slip away. If you think of it as a wave that rolls in and out, you can see how briefly it crests. Don't waste an instant of that time—have a treatment program lined up and waiting. The sooner you catch that wave, the more likely it is your loved one will ride it to success.

Use the drinking maps you have made to figure out when your drinker is most likely to accept treatment and be alert for those windows of opportunity. Then, when the window opens, use your PIUS communication skills to lovingly but firmly present the treatment option. Do so with the expectation that your loved one will agree, but be prepared to back off if you see resistance or anger. Keep that wave image in mind and rest assured that even once the wave has slipped back out to sea, it will eventually return to where you sit waiting for it. Just as each time you fall off a surfboard teaches you a little more about how to stay on it, each time you broach the subject of treatment without an argument, you get a little closer to the time your loved one accepts and enters treatment.

Recap

- Seek treatment programs that have strong empirical support for their effectiveness. We recommend those that use methods described with phrases such as "behavioral," "cognitive behavioral," or "skills training" and that involve the drinker's loved ones in the change effort.
- Have treatment for your loved one lined up and ready to go the minute she agrees to try it.

- Use your road maps to identify the windows of opportunity in which you can suggest treatment with a reasonably good chance that your loved one will be receptive to the idea.

Kathy and Jim: Opening Windows

Good things were happening once Kathy got into the habit of mapping Jim's drinking and *planning in advance* how she would handle different situations. Although he was still drinking a lot, which was still causing problems, there were more evenings that Jim would come straight home from work and spend the evening sober with Kathy. He also had started taking Ted out for pizza and video games on Saturday afternoons as well as spending a little more quality time with the two younger children. On top of that, Kathy had set up a regular date with her sister every Thursday evening, and Jim knew he was expected to be home to watch the kids. He didn't always show up on time (and Kathy would drop the kids off at her mother's or a neighbor's), but he did accept responsibility for the evening.

Life had definitely improved since the days when Kathy felt it was not worth living. However, Jim was still drinking, and even though he enjoyed his afternoons with Ted and accepted responsibility for Thursday evenings with the children, he would still frequently come home drunk or pop open a beer before his scheduled outing with Ted. When that happened, Kathy would not let him drive with the child, and Jim would get angry and storm out of the house to drink. Nonetheless, Kathy felt like she finally had a little control over her life, and Jim had rediscovered some pleasure in his family, which made it easier for her to tempt him to remain sober.

Kathy made a list of the times she thought Jim would be most receptive to entering treatment. Whenever he got drunk instead of taking Ted out on Saturday, Jim would wake up Sunday morning racked with guilt. He would apologize profusely and typically try to abstain all day to atone. Kathy decided this would be a good time to bring up treatment, as would the Friday mornings after the Thursday nights when he'd come home late and drunk to find his kids gone to his mother-in-law's house and a note from Kathy telling him how disappointed the children were.

Having identified these windows of opportunity, Kathy waited for them and prepared. She found a good therapist not far from the house who was willing to juggle her calendar and fit Jim in as soon as he said okay. This woman was a cognitive-behavioral clinical psychologist who focused on helping alcoholics develop the skills needed to turn away from liquor and rebuild their lives. She also insisted that Kathy be prepared to be an active member of the therapy team with Jim. Kathy was thrilled and made a couple of appointments just for herself in the meantime—partly to get to know the therapist and partly to help keep her own spirits up.

When the moment arrived and Jim was apologizing for another ruined Saturday, Kathy said, "Jim, I know you want things to be good for the kids and us. I do too. In fact, I've been seeing this wonderful therapist who has really helped me to manage my feelings. She would love to meet you, and you might find her helpful. I've got an appointment with her tomorrow. You can really make a difference for our family if you come with me and talk to her." Prepared to back off at the slightest sign of anger, Kathy was delighted when Jim asked her if this was a "shrink for crazies" and if she was going to try to mess with his head. Happy to satisfy Jim's curiosity about the psychologist, Kathy explained how they just talk about stuff. "The therapist," she said, "helps me figure out how to get along better with you as well as control my own feelings so I don't fly off the handle and mess things up." Kathy knew this was the very thing Jim had spent the morning apologizing for. Jim agreed to meet the therapist, and Kathy quickly called the answering service to leave a message that they would be in to see her at the pre-agreed time Monday morning.

Kathy was so thrilled and Jim so determined to not act like "a crazy" that the rest of the day was wonderful. He did not drink, and Kathy went out of her way to let Jim know how much she loved him and enjoyed his sober company.

chapter 12

Relapse Prevention

Carlene and Peter

Peter had really cut back his drinking quite a bit over the few months Carlene had been applying her newly learned behavior-change skills and PIUS communication. He had even been attending AA meetings fairly regularly and seemed to be sincere about wanting to kick his drinking habit. Nonetheless, every three or four weeks he would have a particularly bad day at work, or he and Carlene would argue over money, and he would go on a binge. Carlene struggled between wanting to reward his nondrinking behavior and feeling betrayed by the times he did drink. In spite of the fact that things were better, she still worried a lot.

Here we are at the final step. This must be the happily-ever-after part, right? Not quite. Snow White and Prince Charming lived happily-ever-after. The rest of us live in the real world. That means we enjoy good times, work through tough times, and generally keep moving forward one step at a time.

Real life is full of ups and downs, as you well know, and the difference between people who get stuck in the downs and those who do not is in how they *interpret* them. For instance, consider someone whose partner abuses alcohol and

whose life is consumed with surviving in this difficult relationship. This individual can look at the situation and see it
as awful and hopeless and give up hope of ever having a better life. Or the person can look at the situation and see problems that need solving and put energy into figuring out how
to do that. (The second person should sound very familiar at
this point.) In fact, the real winners at life even go so far as to
see problems as *opportunities*. Anytime something goes wrong
or someone messes up, you have the opportunity to learn a
little more about what makes things or people tick by taking
them apart (the behaviors, not the people) and figuring out
what caused the problem.

Lapses

Everybody makes mistakes. Whether you are learning to walk,
trying to lose weight, changing the way you communicate, or
trying to stop abusing alcohol, you will mess up. It is a perfectly natural part of being alive.

When someone is trying to change her behavior and messes
up, we call the mistake a "lapse." *Lapses are an expected part of
the change process.* Lapses can certainly be upsetting, such as
when you find your loved one drunk after three weeks of abstinence or you find yourself slipping back into an old confrontational style of speaking. However, whether the lapse is
an opportunity or a catastrophe is entirely dependent upon
how you look at it.

Every time you and your loved one make plans and those
plans go awry, you each have the opportunity to learn a little
something more about yourselves. Behavior does not occur in
a vacuum, so if you did not follow your planned behaviors, you
know for certain that something triggered you to sidetrack.
Take the time to review the situation in which the lapse oc-

curred and find those triggers. For instance, you had planned a family dinner at your favorite Chinese restaurant, and your son shows up higher than a kite after five weeks of abstinence. Although this feels like a relapse with a capital *R,* you and he can analyze what preceded today's lapse and identify, for instance, girlfriend problems over the past few days with the accompanying depression that lead him to think about how unfair his life is and how he really "needs" to feel better. Perhaps his best friend was out of town, and he didn't have anyone to talk to. You and he may decide that in similar situations in the future, he could call you, his AA sponsor, or his favorite uncle. Whatever the coping strategy you devise, the important thing is that the drinking episode is seen, not as a failure, but as a natural part of the process of learning how to better manage himself. Maintain your focus on the five weeks of sobriety already achieved and the good changes that have resulted. Do not let one day of drinking cast a dark shadow on this wonderful change the two of you have already initiated.

You already know everything you need to turn lapses into learning opportunities. You know how to track your behavior, you know how to map interactions, and you know the importance of planning ahead and rehearsing. All that remains for you to learn, if you have not already, is to control your emotional reaction to a lapse long enough for you to apply your analytical skills.

High-Risk Situations

You can make it easier to avoid an emotional overreaction to a lapse by anticipating and preparing for it. Obviously, you cannot know in advance every situation that will trigger you or your loved one to slip back into old habits, but you can probably predict more of those situations than you might first think. Think about the changes you have made in the way you respond to your loved one getting drunk, and reflect on the situations in which it has been particularly difficult for you to stay with your new pattern. These are your *high-risk situations* for maintaining this new behavior. Activity 23 will help you anticipate your high-risk situations. Carlene found that it was actually pretty easy to predict what types of situations would rattle her the most. Take a look at her following responses and then write your own answers in your notebook.

◆ Activity 23. Identify High-Risk Situations

1. In what mood or moods are you most likely to lapse? *When I'm depressed and feeling sorry for myself. Pretty much any negative emotional state.*
2. At what time of day are you least confident of maintaining your new behavior pattern? *End of the day, after work.*
3. What places make it particularly difficult for you? *Can't think of any.*
4. Are there any people whose presence makes it tough to stay with your new pattern? *When the kids are running around while I'm trying to talk to Peter.*
5. Are there any days of the week or weekend that are particularly difficult? *Can't think of any.*
6. What situations are most likely to make you lose control? *Definitely when he comes home drunk, obviously having driven in that condition.*
7. What moods of your loved one make it especially hard for you to stay in control? *When he's drunk.*
8. What statements or tones of voice of your loved one push your buttons? *That drunken, snarling voice.*
9. What behaviors of your loved one set you off? *Drinking and driving.*

10. Are there times you feel physically unwell that make it tough to stay the course (for example, when you have a headache, are sick, or, if you are female, when you are pre-menstrual)? *Nothing consistent.*

There are as many potential high-risk situations as there are individuals. Moreover, having identified the situations that are high-risk for you today does not mean new ones will not arise next week. (Happily, old ones will eventually lose their power too.) To really stay on top of things, you must continually ask yourself, "*What* sets me up to lapse?" "*Who* is most likely to trigger a lapse?" "*Where* am I most likely to be vulnerable to losing control?" and "*What* thoughts and feelings trigger problems?" Keep in mind that your drinker may not be the person who sets you up to lapse. If you are worn-out from working or frazzled by the kids or relatives, you may be too tired or stressed to deal effectively with your drinker. Anticipate these types of high-risk situations too. They are part of your life so be sure not to overlook them.

You can see that by carefully thinking through all the moods, times, behaviors, and so on that might trigger a lapse, you can identify a number of high-risk situations. Now you can prepare for them. Do so by using the same mapping strategy you used to analyze your drinker's behavior (from chapter 2).

Carlene decided that the most powerful lapse trigger for her was when Peter would drive home drunk, so she mapped out that high-risk situation first and in considerable detail. It looked something like this.

Peter is late getting home, so I know he'll show up drunk. ➔ I mentally review my new-and-improved plans for handling this situation. ➔ He finally shows up and I start to say the PIUS speech I had planned, but he snarls at me and throws his car keys on the counter as he stomps into the bedroom. ➔ I feel uncontrollable anger and even hatred well up in me. ➔ I think about how ungrateful he is and how little he cares about me and the children to not only get plastered like that but to drive our car in that condition. He could wreck the car (where would that leave us?!) and kill himself or land in jail. ➔ I explode and tell him just what a jerk he is.

Even though I know I'm right and he's wrong and he deserves to feel as bad as, or worse than, I feel, I also know that making that point has never helped things in the past and probably won't help now. So I need an action plan to manage this situation. I'll examine each step of this lapse map and plan a new route for as many steps as I can. The more detours I build in to it, the more easily I can still get off this rocky road even if I miss the first turnoff or two. **(Carlene's detours are printed in bold.)**

Peter is late getting home, so I know he'll show up drunk. ➔ I mentally review my new-and-improved plans for handling this situation **and make a list of the positive changes I am working toward and compare the satisfaction I will have from telling him off to that I will have from seeing him change.** ➔ He finally shows up and I start to say the PIUS speech I had planned, but he snarls at me and throws his car keys on the counter as he stomps into the bedroom. ➔ I feel uncontrollable anger and even hatred well up in me, **so I take a deep breath and go into the bathroom where I lock the door and take a few moments to remind myself of what I am trying to accomplish and that a blowup will only ensure we repeat this scene again and again.**

➔ I think about how ungrateful he is and how little he cares about me and the children to not only get plastered like that but to drive our car in that condition. He could wreck the car (where would that leave us?!) and kill himself or land in jail. **I remind myself that alcohol changes a person's brain, and even though he is responsible for his drinking, the behavior that follows drinking is the result of the liquor. He doesn't intentionally try to make our life miserable. I also remind myself of my ultimate goal—getting him sober—not proving my point tonight. ➔ Instead of** "I explode and tell him just what a jerk he is," **I leave the bathroom and say to him, "I know how difficult it is for you to control your drinking, and you know how much it scares me when you drink and drive. Right now it's probably best if we both just got a good night's sleep. In the morning, though, I really want to talk about this stuff. I love you. Good night."**

Once Carlene completed her new map, she took a few moments, two or three times each day, to imagine herself living the situation just as she described it. Not only did she mentally walk through each step, she really tried to feel the feelings she described. She imagined Peter giving her his meanest snarl and stomping past her. She experienced the rising tide of anger and hatred and then actively pictured herself taking a deep breath instead of exploding, going into the bathroom to calm down and think, and so on. This may sound like an awful lot of work for the benefit of a drunken jerk but remember, this is the man she loves, and Carlene believes they can still have a good life together if they just lick this drinking problem. So the effort is worthwhile; it may just be that having Carlene react calmly with love to Peter's best drunken snarl is the straw that tips the scales for him and leaves him feeling guilty and willing to talk about treatment in the morning. Out of the worst situations sometimes come the greatest opportunities.

Surprise Attacks

As prepared as you will be for the high-risk situations you anticipate, some events will still catch you by surprise. That's okay. You cannot predict every trigger, but you can use the unexpected to add to your arsenal. As soon as the dust settles, grab your notebook and describe the whole situation from beginning to end as if you were a detective looking for every tiny clue to solve an important mystery. Write down everything that happened including the players, the setting, what everybody said and did, how you felt, what you said to yourself, the mood of your loved one—everything. Then order it into the sequence in which it occurred and look for spots in the sequence that you could have handled differently and describe how. This becomes your new plan for the situation. Thus, even the worst, most upsetting situations can be a surprise only once. Next time it happens, you will be prepared.

Drinker Lapses

The same approach that you apply to your lapses is appropriate for your loved one to use when she lapses from treatment plans. Our hope is that whatever treatment the two of you opt for, it includes a rational, problem-solving approach to lapses. Unless your loved one is superhuman, you can bet on the fact that lapses will happen. He may remain abstinent for a while and then get drunk or take Antabuse (a medication that causes the individual to become ill if taken with alcohol) faithfully for a while and then stop. Lapses may come in the form of skipping therapy sessions or allowing her temper to erupt violently; you can predict the most likely scenarios better than anyone.

You can help your drinker not let lapses turn into full-blown drinking episodes (relapses) by keeping the same opportunistic outlook about his lapses as you do about your own. Difficult as it will be, you can help your loved one rationally examine each lapse and find the triggers that require better handling. On your own, you can certainly analyze her lapses looking for what you might have done to prevent or minimize them. Although you are not the cause of the problem, always remember you have the power to be part of the solution.

If the two of you are working with a good cognitive-behavioral therapist, you and your loved one will have lots of support to help you deal profitably with lapses. Everyone knows the road to sobriety is not a smooth one, and learning how to maneuver around the potholes is a critical piece of therapy. If your drinker has opted not to enter treatment but tries to beat the problem with just your help, you will need to be especially strong to keep a positive spin on things. It will be especially important for you to have a good support system. So if you have not already set one up, get busy.

Handling Dropouts

People drop out of treatment. Drinkers, in particular, drop out of treatment. Help your loved one enter treatment with the expectation that he will remain long enough to "graduate," but do not be caught unprepared if your loved one quits. Also, do not be devastated. Dropping out does not mean the trip is over. It means you have dropped back a few exits on the freeway, but you are most definitely still on the road.

All the changes you have made to date are still there. You

have improved the quality of your life by expanding your social circle, built rewards into your interactions, and relieved
yourself of the harmful habits of covering up and fixing. You
have even achieved the ultimate success of getting the drinker
to admit treatment makes sense. Having done so once, you
can do so again. Everything you did this time will work again
(with modifications based on experience). There is no question about that. The only question that remains is whether
you want to continue. Think carefully about this one before
you decide. Sometimes your gut tells you to quit because you
are so tired and discouraged, but you are not *really* ready to
give up on your loved one. And other times, it really is time
to quit.

Staying Motivated

Motivation fluctuates. One set of events comes together to
motivate you to make changes—you feel you can climb any
mountain—and then another set of events makes you feel
that even one more step is too much. Sometimes motivation
just seeps away because of hard work and little results.

The changes you have already made are just the beginning
of a long, ongoing process. At times it will be exciting and ex-
hilarating, and at other times it will be discouraging. It can be
especially difficult to stay motivated when you feel like you
are the one doing all the work and your drinker is not helping at all. When you start thinking like that, it is easy to run
out of steam. However, there are things you can do to help
yourself stay motivated.

Keep One Eye on the Goal

When those adventurous people who climb high, snow-
capped mountains are slogging through the ice and cold, they
keep themselves motivated and alive by keeping one eye on

that lofty peak and the other on the details of staying alive and moving forward. You know what you are hoping to accomplish with all this work, and you have already decided that it is worth the work. Remind yourself daily (hourly if need be) of where you are trying to go. Review the notes you made in earlier activities and spend a little time dreaming. Keep your eye on your goal and it will make the effort to get there feel a little less intense.

Keep One Eye on the Details

It may be a long time before your life resembles your goal in a big way. However, each day that you make little changes, you do move closer to that dream. Continue to track all your plans, attempts, and outcomes, and reward yourself for every effort. Those are the details that create success. Count them!

Figure Your Investment

When you are fed up and feel like giving up, take a minute to review how much you have already put into this relationship. The time, the energy, the love you have invested can eventually yield a good outcome. But it does take time and, typically, ongoing investments. If you pull out prematurely, you not only lose the possibility of ever realizing your goals, but you also lose the investment you have already made. As long as your goal has great value for you, the investment will not be too great.

Get By with a Little Help from Your Friends

Don't forget that you have people who can help. Those folks who you have taken into your confidence can offer a tremendous amount of support. From role-playing with you, to giving you pep talks, to merely sharing a quiet cup of coffee, they can provide the soothing and nurturing needed to ease your discouragement and let your motivation peak again. Do not sabotage yourself by assuming that no one will want to help. Most people get pleasure out of being able to help others, so think of your request for help as something nice you are doing for a friend. You are giving your friend the opportunity to do something that makes her feel good.

Rely on Your Community

If you need more support than your social circle can provide, check out community support groups for people in your situation. Almost every community in the country has Twelve Step group meetings you can attend to share your burden with others who carry a similar weight. Calling local religious organizations, the YMCA, the local veterans center, or community clinics will also often turn up groups that interest you and can help you through this period. As we have repeatedly pointed out, you are not alone. Alcohol abuse is almost a national pastime, so there are many others in the same situation as you—loving a drinker and wanting more out of life. Those people can be a tremendous source of understanding, support, and motivation.

When to Quit

Everyone who learns the *Alternatives* wins. You either win by seeing your loved one break free of alcohol, or you win by satisfying yourself that you have done everything possible and have the right to live the life you choose. The big question, of course, becomes—when do you decide you have done everything you possibly can? To help you decide, ask yourself the following questions:

- Have I as consistently as I could mapped out problem situations and planned more effective, non-confrontational behaviors for myself?

- Have I practiced a PIUS communication style?
- Have I kept track of how my plans went and adjusted them based on those experiences?
- Have I stopped acting as my loved one's caretaker and allowed him to experience the real consequences of drinking?
- Have I rewarded my loved one for nondrinking behavior and made it as enjoyable as possible to be sober with me and/or the family?
- Have I added pleasurable activities to my own life so that I am not totally absorbed by the drinking problems?
- Have I figured out when the best windows of opportunity to suggest treatment are and planned how I will use them?
- Have I lined up a reasonable treatment option and made it available to my loved one?
- Is there anything that I thought might help and I meant to do but didn't?
- Can I see an attractive future with this person?
- Once I get over missing my loved one, will a future without her bring me greater peace and happiness than one with her?

As you answer these questions, remember: **You deserve to be happy.** No one has to earn happiness by suffering. When you have done everything you can to improve life with your drinker and nothing has improved, it may be time to consider life without him. We know the pain that comes with thinking of giving up this relationship you have worked so very hard to preserve, but we also know the pain that comes with continuing to beat your head against a brick wall. We have seen it too often. When you have done everything you can, you owe it to yourself to turn your focus entirely on you and any other family members for whom you are responsible. You all deserve a life free of fear, free of anger, and free of alcohol. That life will be yours, either with your drinker or without. Your decision is the right one.

Action Summary

As you move forward, remember that the road we travel is a changing one. Sometimes it is smooth, and sometimes it is ravaged by potholes (lapses). Staying on course depends on your willingness to work around those obstacles. They are a natural part of this process and can actually make you stronger as you use them to figure out what went wrong and what went right. Moving toward your ultimate goal, the life you want to live with your loved one, is a meandering process. In many cases it is possible. And when it proves too difficult to achieve, you can turn off the road comfortable that you have done everything you can to keep the relationship together. In either case, you can create a life that feels right for you—with or without your drinker. You deserve it.

Recap

- Lapses, or mistakes, are a natural part of life. Thus, they are to be expected in any change process.
- High-risk situations are those circumstances in which lapses are more likely to occur.
- By analyzing the circumstances in which lapses occur and problem-solving new means of handling those circumstances, you can use even periods of frequent lapsing to strengthen your ability to move toward your goals.

Kathy and Jim: Looking to the Future

Kathy was as nervous as she could ever imagine being when she and Jim went to see the psychologist. She was afraid the doctor would anger Jim by pushing too hard, or Jim would show up in one of his screw-the-world moods. By the time they got to the office, Kathy was wiping her sweaty palms on her slacks. "What's with you?" Jim wanted to know. Kathy replied that she so much wanted things to work out well for them that she was really nervous about the visit. She didn't want to upset him, she said. Jim patted her hand and reminded her that if he didn't like it, he knew he didn't have to go back, so no big deal.

The visit consisted of the psychologist asking Jim about his relationship with Kathy and what he liked and didn't like about the way they lived. She also asked him if he ever worried about his drinking and how he thought his life might be different if he drank less. At first, Jim was a little hesitant to speak but soon warmed up and really got into exploring things with the therapist. At the end of the session, he agreed to come back the following week to continue helping with "Kathy's" therapy.

That evening when Jim and Kathy met back at home after work, she thanked him again for coming and told Jim how much his participation meant to her. Jim felt pretty good about the situation; it had been a long time since he felt like he could contribute to Kathy's happiness. She was elated. She knew that the road ahead still held many potholes, but at last, she knew they were on the right road.

References

Ellis, B. H., I. McCan, G. Price, and C. M. Sewell. 1992. The New Mexico treatment outcome study: Evaluating the utility of existing information systems. *Journal of Health Care for the Poor and Underserved* 3, no. 1:138–50.

Johnson, V. E. 1986. *Intervention: How to help those who don't want help.* Minneapolis, Minn.: Johnson Institute.

Meyers, R. J., and J. E. Smith. 1995. *Clinical guide to alcohol treatment: The community reinforcement approach.* New York: Guilford Press.

Meyers, R. J., W. R. Miller, D. E. Hill, and J. S. Tonigan. 1999. Community reinforcement and family training (CRAFT): Engaging unmotivated drug users in treatment. *Journal of Substance Abuse* 10, no. 3:291–308.

Meyers, R. J., W. R. Miller, J. E. Smith, and J. S. Tonigan. 2002. A randomized trial of two methods for engaging treatment-refusing drug users through concerned significant others. *Journal of Consulting and Clinical Psychology* 70, no. 5:1182–85.

Miller, W. R., and R. K. Hester. 1986. Inpatient alcoholism treatment: Who benefits? *American Psychologist* 41:794–805.

Miller, W. R., R. J. Meyers, and J. S. Tonigan. 1999. Engaging the unmotivated in treatment for alcohol problems: A comparison of three intervention strategies. *Journal of Consulting and Clinical Psychology* 67, no. 5:688–97.

Nowinski, J. K. 1998. *Family recovery and substance abuse: A twelve-step guide for treatment.* Thousand Oaks, Calif.: Sage Publications.

Index

About the Authors

Robert J. Meyers, Ph.D., is research associate professor of psychology at the University of New Mexico. He is also the associate director of the LifeLink Training Institute in Sante Fe, New Mexico. Dr. Meyers has worked in the substance abuse field for over twenty-seven years and has published several books and dozens of articles. He is well-known for his charismatic training and workshops on a variety of subjects. He is one of the originators of the Community Reinforcement Approach (CRA) for outpatient treatment and the creator of Community Reinforcement and Family Training (CRAFT).

Brenda L. Wolfe, Ph.D., is a clinical psychologist. In addition to her busy private practice, Dr. Wolfe is involved in research collaborations at the University of New Mexico, serves as a corporate consultant for the development of psychologically based services, and is active in various professional organizations. Her books and articles have appeared in both the popular and professional press.

Hazelden Publishing and Educational Services is a division of the Hazelden Foundation, a not-for-profit organization. Since 1949, Hazelden has been a leader in promoting the dignity and treatment of people afflicted with the disease of chemical dependency.

The mission of the foundation is to improve the quality of life for individuals, families, and communities by providing a national continuum of information, education, and recovery services that are widely accessible; to advance the field through research and training; and to improve our quality and effectiveness through continuous improvement and innovation.

Stemming from that, the mission of this division is to provide quality information and support to people wherever they may be in their personal journey—from education and early intervention, through treatment and recovery, to personal and spiritual growth.

Although our treatment programs do not necessarily use everything Hazelden publishes, our bibliotherapeutic materials support our mission and the Twelve Step philosophy upon which it is based. We encourage your comments and feedback.

The headquarters of the Hazelden Foundation are in Center City, Minnesota. Additional treatment facilities are located in Chicago, Illinois; Newberg, Oregon; New York, New York; Plymouth, Minnesota; St. Paul, Minnesota; and West Palm Beach, Florida. At these sites, we provide a continuum of care for men and women of all ages. Our Plymouth facility is designed specifically for youth and families.

For more information on Hazelden, please call **1-800-257-7800.** Or you may access our World Wide Web site on the Internet at **www.hazelden.org.**